CROCHET

FOR BEGINNERS

*The Ultimate Step by Step Handbook
with Illustrations and Instructions to Learn
Crocheting in a Quick and Easy Way*

Gemma Stone

Table of Contents

Introduction

Crocheting is a hobby that is ever-increasing in popularity, and this is for a wide range of reasons! Not only is it fun to create your own clothing, homewares and toys, and a brilliant way to express your creativity, it is also relaxing, entertaining and often it creates a strong bond with friends or family if you decide to collaborate on a project. Crocheting is an amazingly useful skill to have and not too challenging to come to grips with, and reading this guide will give you all the tools you need to master it within three short days – what better way could you spend your time?

Crochet is derived from the French word meaning 'hook,' and it's the procedure of producing fabric from the thread, yarn, or additional material strands by means of a crochet hook. These hooks can be made from metals, woods or plastic. The process of crocheting is similar to that of knitting in that it consists of pulling loops of material through other loops. It differs from knitting because only one stitch is active at a time, and it uses the hook rather than knitting needles, which creates a wide variety of unique stitches, allowing you to create some very special products. Many people find crocheting easier to master as it only uses one primary tool, but this simplicity allows you to become much more creative with your designs.

If you are looking forward to learning how to crochet, then this is the best book for you. This book will give you a step-by-step guide and will teach you the techniques and benefits of crocheting. The book will introduce you to the tools for crochet, the yarns, the hook, and the types of crochets. You will be able to learn how to hold the hook and the yarn and then proceed to the techniques and stitches. In the end, you will be able to come up with successful projects that will motivate you even further into trying some amazing patterns.

The art of Crocheting attracts many people. It's one of the simplest ways to express your creativity. As a result, when you go online, you will definitely get plenty of books on crocheting. I would like to thank you again for choosing this one! We put all our efforts into it to ensure that it contains as much useful information as possible. Have fun and enjoy it!

Why Do You Need to Crochet?

Learning how to crochet provides the most amazing experience. Rather than just spending your time on phones or other electronic devices, you can spend it on coming up with something more useful. Crocheting allows you to express your creativity. You will have wide options for color choices and designs, and the way you will use them will express your ideas and thoughts.

By simply coming up with amazing designs, you will develop or boost your self-esteem because it will give you some sense of pride and the desire to achieve even much greater.

Teaching children how to crochet can be very useful: it will help them to understand how to follow instructions, besides they will be able to learn how to read, how to recognize different colors, they will be even able to improve their mathematics skills through different crochet patterns.

CHAPTER 1:

Amazing Benefits of Crochet

Many people crochet to pass the time. If you are in this category, you should know that you are doing yourself a lot of good. Not only does the time you spend making several designs help you to reduce accumulated body stress and anxiety, but it also helps you to:

Feel fulfilled. You get to give yourself a pat on the back when you are done with a particular project. Imagine creating something from just a hook and yarn?

Relieve depression. Now, there is something creative and constructive that you are thinking about. You will have less or no time for destructive and depressive thoughts. It has been proved that doing something you like doing makes the brain secrete hormones such as dopamine and serotonin. Dopamine works like an anti-depressant, making you feel good.

Be happy. Crochet works are beautiful when well-done. You'll be happy to be the brain behind a beautiful piece of artwork.

You might make some extra income from it. Especially when people have to work two or three jobs to make ends meet, selling beautiful crochet pieces might be a source of income for the crocheter.

Slow down or prevent memory loss altogether. Memory loss can be slowed down when one partakes in logical exercises, such as crochet.

Also, it helps you to develop fine motor skills. People who have arthritis might do well to consider picking up crocheting as a hobby. It will help to keep their fingers nimble. The craft of crocheting will make you more patient. There is no rushing it, really. It can only be done with the hands, so it will help you learn that some things take time. Working on stitches over time will also help you have a sense of focus and pay attention to detail. Not paying attention to detail might lead to frogging.

The list is almost endless, actually, but let's focus more on the bone of contention—what do you need to crochet successfully?

Clothing can be made in different ways, and one of them is crochet. Some of the other methods include weaving, bonding, and the one closely related to crochet, knitting. Crochet has, however, evolved from the process of making just clothing to making other decorative stuff. This means that you might not want to make a crochet dress for your baby, but you can decorate her nursery with crochet stuff. And why not make her a crochet dress anyway? I can bet that it will surely look good on her.

Crotchet is an enjoyable way out of boredom. There is no need to be idle anymore as you can make something beautiful during your free moments. You can take a leave from work, and while you enjoy your favorite movies on Zee World, hold a hook and yarn in your hands and make a cozy blanket.

A definition of what crochet is might be a great way to start. You should be able to define what you do, right?

To an informed eye, knitted and crochet works are just the same thing. However, knitting isn't the same thing as crochet. They are two different things.

Crochet seems to take less time as compared to knitting. Taking a keen look at both, crochet stitches usually take the form of a knotted look, while knits seem as if you arranged so many 'Vs.' in a straight line.

That's ultimately your choice to make, though. Knitting and crochet are both yarn crafts and require some time to finish. But if you find out you are not very patient and don't like making mistakes, especially one that will take a longer time to correct, I will surely advise you to take up crochet and ditch knitting (or at least in the meantime).

If you like to express your creativity in your patterns and don't want to spend much money on supplies, you are better off with crochet (even with your fingers and some yarn, you are good to go!).

Yarns can be classified based on their raw materials. This could be natural products (plants and animal sources) or human-made (synthetic). Natural yarns could be alpaca, wool, cotton, bamboo, silk, cashmere, or linen.

Synthetic yarns could be made from polyester, acrylic, or nylon fibers.

There is also a third category, the blended yarn, which is made from a combination of natural and synthetic fibers.

Let's talk about three of the types as they are fit for beginners in crochet.

Acrylic yarn. I guess this is the most common type of yarn. It is affordable and fairly easy to maintain and will still look good after long use. It can be a great starting material for a blanket. The use of acrylic yarn is not limited to crochet; it can be used for other purposes, e.g., hair extensions.

Cotton. As a material, is lightweight, and the same goes for cotton yarns. Baby clothes can be made from cotton yarns as well as other intended light-weighted crochet works.

Wool. This is rather bulky so that it can be great for cold weather. You can use it to crochet cardigans, hats, etc. Wool is also great for a beginner crocheter because of its size.

Please note that the instruction will most likely specify the yarn to use. In cases where it is not specified, you can follow the guidelines above.

However, if you are a beginner, you can use any yarn you are okay with (brightly colored and bulky, though). Once you master it, you can switch learning to practice with other yarn types. This is because different crochet patterns require different yarn types.

CHAPTER 2:

The History of Crochet

We do not know many things regarding the early origins of crochet because the ancient textiles that survived are very few. Some claim that originally, women used fingers to create loops and chains.

Only later did they begin to use a tool very similar to the current hook, which was initially made of wood, bone, or bamboo and then in ivory and amber.

The oldest find, considered a precursor of crochet, comes from Jutland. It is a woolen cap that dates to about 3100 years ago. However, primitive textile samples were found in every corner of the globe—Far East, Asia, North and South America, and Europe.

Some scholars believe that Tambour's work was at the origin of modern crochet. This technique was used in China. It required the use of a fine hook to weave threads through a netted background.

This technique arrived in France around 1720.

An American scholar, Mary Thomas, believes that crochet work originally comes from the Arabian Peninsula. From here, it spread eastward, in Tibet, and to the west, in Spain and then, thanks to merchants and sailors, even in other parts of the world.

The most delicate crochet form originated in Italy in the 16th century and was used by the sisters for making ornaments and vestments. It was considered a typical occupation within the monasteries where sisters created precious lace using very thin yarns. The linen for the altars was fitted with crocheted borders not only for decorative purposes but also to make it more durable. Very soon, it spread to Spain and Ireland, which were very Catholic countries.

Only in the 19th century did crochet begin to be appreciated in the bourgeoisie and the noble. The laces were used to adorn the linen of the house and underwear. Lace, finished with precious scallops full of picots and various decorations, had a huge development, especially among the ladies of the bourgeoisie, and they adorned their precious clothes with collars, gaskets and tippets.

The crochet, which until then was not considered a genre, developed to mimic the difficult points of Venetian lace. The work was faster than needle and bobbin lace, and tools were simpler and easier to find.

Perhaps its popularity took off from a lady of French origin, Eleonore Riego de la Branchardiere, who settled in Ireland, where she remained impressed by the delicacy of the work of the nuns in a convent in Dublin. She not only perfected their skills but spoke of the art of crochet in her magazine "The Needle." She also published eleven books in which contained conversion tables from needle lace and bobbin lace to crochet.

She is commonly credited with the invention of the Irish Lace. When times were hard, women had to find ways of supporting their families. This was particularly true during and after the great potato famine of the 1840s when crochet became the sole economic support. Another factor that contributed to the spread of crochet was the creation of a kind of domestic industry born in Clones to help the poorest families, thanks to Cassandra Hand, the wife of a local parish priest. The Clones Lace, still widely known, is a variant of Venetian lace. The Venetian lace, although very beautiful, required considerable time and Irish women found that by using the crochet hook, they could achieve the same effect in less time. These women reproduced elements linked to their environment: shamrocks, fern, brambles, wild roses, daisies, or star-shaped figures.

When Queen Victoria promoted the crochet lace in an exhibition of Arts in London, fashion took off. Soon, demand became so high that professional sellers took the place of charities, and the activity of lace turned from survival activities into an industry. The patterns of crocheted lace began to be written and distributed. Irish girls traveled to other parts of the world to teach crocheted lace. From the Irish Lace came the Orvieto lace, which, over the years, has acquired a peculiarity and original identity. In 1907, the Ars Wattana, a "patronage for young workers," was born. It sought to carry out the activity of production and packaging of lace and frill with special ornamental details for the Duomo of Orvieto, aimed at strengthening and developing local crafts.

The popularity of crochet reached its peak between 1910 and 1920, with the fashion of the Edwardian era. Its models were more complex stitches and the prevalence of white yarn. They began to be printed in series of books with crochet patterns that took the place of honor in the decoration and creation of clothes and household items.

In 1930, fashion acquired simpler features. Art Deco was the trend of the moment, and crochet was used primarily for garments of children and infants, christening gowns, gloves, and blankets. During the Second World War, yarn was rationed, and since crocheting wastes more yarn than knitting, crochet seemed to be doomed. Even though crochet was all the rage in Europe, it had not really gained much popularity in America. Most women who crocheted were immigrants who loved the availability of ready-made threads and other materials.

After the turn of the century, America finally accepted crochet, and it became part of the many skills taught to young girls. It was considered a leisure activity since it did not produce a functional or marketable good. It was pretty much reserved for the middle and upper classes. In the 60s, crochet came back strongly in vogue after a long hibernation, using the vivid colors of granny squares.

Crochet's popularity continued to grow until the 70s, with ponchos being the must-have accessories.

In the 80s, crochet began to fall out of favor. The economy was growing, and more women were working, thus having less time for crafts. Plus, crochet work was no longer affordable.

Crochet and knitting lost their importance even in the school curriculum—nobody taught it anymore, and the new generation had no time to learn. This time, it seemed that crochet was really facing extinction.

Fortunately, since the middle of the 90s, crochet has experienced a new period of interest. Crochet can be seen today as a hobby, but for those who have awareness, they consider it an art form.

CHAPTER 3:

How to Read and Understand Crochet

Perhaps, the main thing in crochet is realizing how to peruse the example. American and English examples are regularly composed, while in Japan or different nations, they will be drawn. The last mentioned, opposed to utilizing words, utilizes a pictorial graph like the one that appeared beneath.

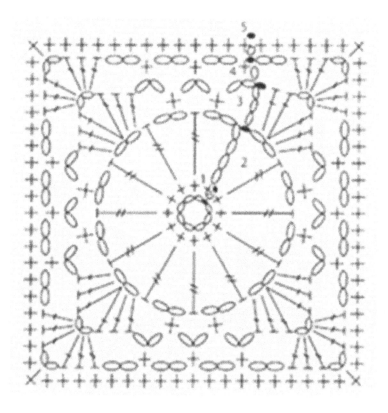

In the event that you are a knitter, you are most likely acquainted with booked work; nonetheless, crochet outlines are drawn instead of diagramed.

Crochet graphs are utilized for a wide range of undertakings and can, with a touch of training, be more functional and successful than composed directions. Today, more creators are settling on graphs or are including the two outlines and composed directions.

For an intricate outline, you may need to likewise utilize a line counter. A column counter permits you to snap or move a dab to follow the number of lines you've finished. While this isn't normally fundamental for a little diagram, it very well may be exceptionally useful for bigger outlines.

Most examples start with a progression of circles, likewise called chains or a slip line. In any case, you can undoubtedly figure out how to make an establishment without utilizing a standard chain. Tasks are ordinarily worked in columns wherein you need to switch to and fro, with each line over the past line. You can likewise join in rounds wherein you work around a ring of chains and make a mathematical figure; for example, a circle, hexagon, or square. You can likewise utilize a theme or a mathematical piece to fasten together and structure your crochet project.

The first is the most common and will be found in vintage designs, just as numerous advanced American and British examples. This is a completely worked-out join design, utilizing regular and conventional line documentation.

Charts are considerably more regularly utilized for doilies or wraps, instead of straightforward undertakings, similar to a cap or afghan, and they are infrequently utilized for rehashed line designs yet can be.

Composed crochet designs are as yet the most well-known in America and Britain. They are generally simple to utilize, and design documentation is, to a great extent, normalized.

An illustration of a composed model is the accompanying: make a chain of any length wanted, in addition to 3 joins for turning.

Row 1: make 5 DC in the third st from the end, * skirt 2 ch, make 1 SC in next join, avoid 2, and make 5 DC in next fasten. *

Row 2: Ch. 3, and turn. Work 4 DC into SC * 1 SC into third DC of the past line, 5 DC into SC of the past line. Rehash from * across the column.

Repeat row 2 to the ideal length.

We should investigate this in a worked-out structure:

Row 1: make 5 twofold crochet fastens in the third join from the finish of the chain. *Skip 2 chains, make one, the crochet ought to be single the following join, skirt 2 chains and make 5 twofold crochet lines in the following stitch. *

Row 2: chain 3 and turn. Work 4 twofold crochet into single crochet.

Work one the crochet. It ought to be single to third twofold crochet of the past line, 5 twofold crochet into the single crochet of the last column.

Repeat from * to end.

With simply a little practice, the shortened forms will turn out to be natural.

British Notation	American Notation
double crochet (dc)	single crochet (sc)
half treble (htr)	half double crochet (hdc)
treble (tr)	double crochet (dc)
double treble (dtr)	treble (tr)
triple treble (trtr)	double treble (dtr)
miss	skip
tension	gauge
yarn over hook (yoh)	yarn over (yo)

An example of a model based on the Pythagorean diagram is the following:

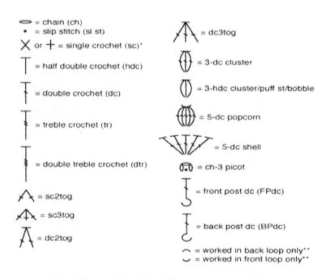

The actual images are all-inclusive, yet notice that the language alludes to American crochet documentation and work the join in like manner.

When amassed to frame a diagram, the images may seem as though you see something about this graph immediately. It makes a visual very much like the completed work, making it simple to understand that your task should resemble, regardless of whether you don't have an image of the completed work.

Round 1: ch 16, get together with a sl st.

Round 2: ch 3, work one dc in the main chain of the last round. *work one dc in next fasten, 2 dc in next around* get together with a sl st. (24)

Round 3: ch 3, sk 1 dc, sc in next, *ch 3, sk 1 dc, SC in next* get together with an sl st.

Round 4: ch 3, *1 dc in first sc, sk 1 ch, *10 dc in second ch line, sk 1 ch, 1 SC in sc* to last ch 3 circles. 9 dc in second ch st, sl st to join to the third ch in starting ch 3.

Round 5: sc in the sixth dc of last dc group, ch 5, dc in sc of prev round, ch5, *sc in the sixth dc of the bunch, ch10, dc in sc of prev round, ch 5, dc in sc of prev round, ch5* get together with sl st.

Round 6: working in reverse to turn around heading, slip join in the initial 5 ch fastens to one side of your snare. This profits you to the edge of your work. Ch 8, sc in the third ch of ch 5 of the last round. *Ch 5 sc in the third ch of ch 5 of the last round. Ch5, dc 3 in the sixth ch of ch 10 of prev round, ch 3, dc3 in the equivalent space*. On the last rehash, dc 2, utilizing the initial 3 chains of introductory chain 8 to make the third dc. Get together with sl st at the third chain.

Round 7: working in reverse once more, sl st in the initial 5 fastens to arrive at the edge of your work. Ch 8, sc in the third ch of ch 5 of the last round. *Ch 5 sc in the third ch of ch 5 of the last round. Ch5, sc in the third ch of ch 5 of prev round, dc 3 in the sixth ch of ch 10 of prev round, ch 3, dc3 in same space*. On the last rehash, dc 2, utilizing the initial 3 chains of introductory chain 8 to make the third dc. Get together with sl st at the third chain.

Round 8: working in reverse once more, sl st in the initial 5 fastens to arrive at the edge of your work. Ch 8, sc in the third ch of ch 5 of the last round. *Ch 5 sc in the third ch of ch 5 of the last round. Ch5, sc in the third ch of ch 5 of prev round, Ch5, sc in the third ch of ch 5 of prev round, dc 3 in the sixth ch of ch 10 of prev round, ch 3, dc3 in same space*.

On the last rehash, dc 2, utilizing the initial 3 chains of beginning chain 8 to make the third dc. Get together with sl st at a third chain.

Crochet Terms and Abbreviations

Alt: substitute.

Ask: implies starting, as the start of the column.

Bp: signifies "back post" like as opposed to working through the circles, you are working the fasten around the post. You regularly pair it with the shortening of the fasten you are utilizing. For instance, bpdc represents back post twofold crochet while bpsc represents back post single crochet.

BL: alludes to the "back circle" crochet. It may likewise be viewed as BLO "back circle as it were." Occasionally, BL can likewise be utilized to allude to bobbles or squares, explicit to the example utilizing it. For this data, check the line rundown of the example that is generally found toward the start of the example BO: bobble.

Cl: group. Your example ought to determine the sort of bunch being utilized, as there are various kinds of groups. For example, 3 tr bunch alludes to a group of 3 high pitch crochet join.

Ch(s): chain(s). This is quite possibly the most widely recognized shortenings you will see since practically all crochet designs start with chains. Most examples likewise incorporate chains all through the plan.

Dtr: twofold high pitch crochet.

Dec: decline. It's a procedure utilized for molding in crochet.

Dc: twofold crochet. It's one of the most well-known fundamental crocheting fastens.

Incl: comprehensive/including/incorporate.

Inc: increment. It's another method utilized in forming, similar to dec (diminishing) is utilized.

Hdc or half dc: half twofold crochet. Its fundamental crochet fastens in the middle of twofold crochet and single crochet in stature.

Fp: front post, when contrasted with "back post."

FL: front circle. It is likewise contracted as FLO (front circle just) rather than BL/BLO as prior referenced.

Oz: ounce(s). It's probably going to be found in the piece of the examples of crocheting, clarifying how much yarn is required or on yarn marks. It might likewise be estimated, for example, yards (yd), meters (m), or grams (g).

Pm: place marker.

Pc: popcorn. A finished crochet line that is like bobbles and groups.

Examples that utilization these sorts of fastens ordinarily clarify how the fashioner needs to make the join toward the start of the example, where the crochet shortening liked by the planner will likewise be seen.

Rem: remaining.

RS: right side. At the point when worked in columns, crochet has both right side and wrong side.

Rnd(s): round(s). They are utilized for including when working in the round or in any case working around and around (rather than working in lines).

Rev: switch. It is regularly utilized along with different shortened forms, for example, fire up sc, which means turn around single crochet fastens.

Rep: rehash. It is habitually positioned along with images that show the piece of the example that will be rehashed.

Models:

[]: the example determines the occasions to rehash a progression of directions given inside the sections.

(): the example determines the occasions to rehash a progression of directions given inside the enclosures.

*: the example determines the occasions to rehash a progression of directions given between indicators or following a bullet.

St(s): stitch (es).

Sp(s): space (s).

Sl st: slip fasten. It's the strategy utilized in joining adjusts when crocheting, just as a line that is utilized all alone.

Sk: skip. For example, you can avoid the following chain and work into the one following, which will be shown by the term sk ch (skip chain).

Sc: single crochet. It is quite possibly the most essential and habitually utilized crochet fastens.

approx	approximately
beg	beginning
blo	back loop only
cc	contrast color
ch	chain
cl	cluster
cont	continue
dc	double crochet
dec	decrease
ea	each
gm	grams
gr	group
hdc	half double crochet
hk	hook
inc	increase
incl	including
lp	loop

Tr: triple crochet/high pitch crochet. It's another fundamental crochet join tr: triple high pitch crochet. Another tall crochet join is significantly taller than the dtr depicted before.

Frock: together. It is now and then used to supplant "decline" where it very well may be composed as "sc2tog" to mean a lessening in single crochet fasten WS = wrong side. It's something contrary to the correct side (rs) as prior depicted.

WIP: work in advancement.

Yoh: yarn over the snare.

YO: yarn over. A stage utilized in making most crochet lines. It's commonly not found in crochet designs yet is frequently found in crochet fasten instructional exercises.

mc	main color
pat	pattern
rem	remaining
rep	repeat
rnd(s)	round(s)
RS	right side
sc	single crochet
sl	slip
slst	slip stitch
sk	skip
sp	space
st(s)	stitch(es)
tog	together
tr / tc	triple (treble) crochet
WS	wrong side
yo	yarn over

CHAPTER 4:

Types of Crochet

When we talk about yarn, most people assume it is only meant for knitting. Not to mention, many people think knitting and crocheting are the same. Knitting and crocheting have the same distinctions, especially when it comes to the tools needed to crochet.

Crocheting has its very own finishes, tools, and techniques, and none of this can be achieved through knitting.

As beginners, it is also good to know the different types of crochet that exist in our world. Take note that crocheting was not a thing in Europe or America. Different variations existed in different parts of the world to be used for a variety of uses, from bags to traditional headgear, clothing, bracelets, adornments, as well as home decor.

Here is a list of 21 well-known crocheting types that still exist in the world and are being practiced everywhere:

Amigurumi Crochet

This is the most popular form of crochet, and its country of origin is Japan. Amigurumi refers to the art of creating small, stuffed toys or objects from crocheted yarn. Amigurumi means to crochet or even to knit, whereas nuigurumi refers to stuffed dolls. Whenever you see a doll or toy made of yarn, it is most likely amigurumi. Many popular culture items have been used to make amigurumi, such as Hello Kitty, Mario Brothers, Pokémon, and Winnie the Pooh.

Aran Crochet

This type of crochet is usually cabled or ribbed. It has its roots in Celtic culture and features interlocking cables. It is often the choice of crochet used for making bigger items such as scarves, sweaters, and beanies. If you see the word 'Aran' in your patterns, be careful because Aran is also used to describe the weight of yarn. Cozy blankets and throws are usually made using Aran crochet.

Items made using Aran crochet:

- Blankets
- Jackets
- Coats
- Scarves
- Throws

Bavarian Crochet

This Bavarian type of crochet is a vintage crochet stitch, and it is traditionally used in rounds. The resulting piece is often a thick fabric that procures for smooth and blended color changes compared to sharp color changes such as the ones commonly seen in a granny square. With Bavarian crochet, you will work in two parts. The first part is the base of clusters, whereas the second part is followed by a row of shells. The Bavarian crochet is the fancier cousin to the granny square.

Items made using Bavarian crochet:

- Blankets
- Shawls
- Tabletop covers

Bosnian Crochet

This type of crochet has a knit-like fabric and is quite dense. It is crocheted using a slip stitch and crocheted in different parts from the row before. Bosnian crochet also uses a different type of hook, conveniently called Bosnian crochet hook, which you can buy, but using regular hooks can work just as well. This type of crochet is called Shepherd's knitting since it also looks like knitted fabrics.

Items made using Bosnian crochet:

- Scarves
- Beanies
- Socks
- Hand gloves

Bullion Crochet

This crochet is a specialized stitch and is achieved using a combination of multiple yarn wraps on a long crochet hook. The result is a distinctive roll stitch, which appears unique too. Motifs are usually made using bullion crochet, and it results in a uniform, thick, and round motif style piece.

Items made using Bullion crochet:

- Stiff items such as placemats
- Motifs for decoration

Broomstick Crochet

Also known as jiffy lace, broomstick crochet is a type of vintage crochet stitch, which is made with a traditional crochet hook. The resulting stitches are formed around a long and wide object such as a broomstick handle, which is how it gets its name. Modern people who crochet use larger crochet hooks or even thick dowels when doing broomstick crochet. This type of crochet is an excellent skill to learn and master as its final product is very beautiful and unique.

Items made using Broomstick crochet:

- Delicate shawls
- Throw blankets for decoration

Bruges Crochet

Ribbons of crochet can be created using this type. These ribbons are then crocheted together, and the results show an intricate lace pattern. This is also the most common type of crochet used in home decor items.

Items made using Bruges crochet:

- Intricate shawls
- Embellishments for clothing
- Tablecloths

Clothesline Crochet

In this crochet style, traditional crochet stitches are done over a clothesline or thick rope or even thick twine to make baskets and circular mats to hold their shape. This type of crocheting can be traced back to Africa and Nepal.

Items made using clothesline crochet:

- Baskets
- Mats
- Structural wall hanging

Clones Lace Crochet

This type of crochet is associated with Irish lace crochet. It was created to be an alternative to the Irish lace crochet because it's easier and quicker to make than the Irish needlepoint lace. The clones knot used for this type of crocheting requires a unique crochet skillset. Clone's lace is a very practical crochet style, and it was commonly used during wars since it was quick and fast to make.

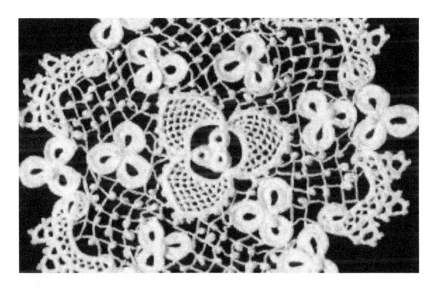

Items made using clones lace crochet:

- Open weave scarves
- Delicate dresses and tops

Cro-hook Crochet

This uniquely named crochet is created using a double-ended hook to create double-sided crochet. This enables you to make stitches in or out at either end of the crochet piece, and this piece does not have a wrong or right side to work on. Because of its nature, this type of crochet is called the Cro-hook or the Cro-knit. This type of crochet closely resembles Tunisian crochet and is an excellent option if you're working with colors that aren't manageable with other types of crochet.

Items made using cro-hook crochet:

- Washcloths
- Scarves
- Baby blankets

Filet Crochet

This style is created using chain rows and double crochet stitches. What you get is a grid-like pattern wherein the squares are either filled or not filled, and the negative space is usually there to create images with the pieces. The wonderful thing about this type of crochet is that you can be completely creative and embed images using empty or full squares of fabric.

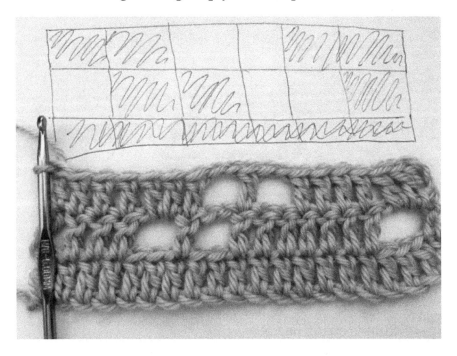

Items made using filet crochet:

- Baby blankets
- Jackets and kimonos
- Handbags
- Cushions

Finger Crochet

This type of crochet is called as such because it does not require hooks. It is similar to finger knitting. It's basically hand fabric that you can use to weave crochet stitches. This is a fun crochet to do when you are a beginner, but the resulting piece has loose tension, which is probably why people move on to hooks to make more versatile projects.

Items made using finger crochet:

- Simple string bags
- Basic scarves

Freeform Crochet

This type of crochet is called freeform because there is no pattern or plan to follow. It is entirely up to the person crocheting to create something. This type of crochet is very artistic and organic, making it an excellent option for beginners. However, if you find yourself struggling without instructions or even a plan, then it's best to avoid freeform and follow crochet pieces with patterns.

Items made using freeform crochet:

- One-off clothing items
- Art pieces

Hairpin Crochet

Like the broomstick crochet, the hairpin crochet is made using the traditional crochet hook, but instead of a broomstick, the piece is held taut using thin metal rods. In earlier times, this technique used actual hairpins, which is how it got its name. The resulting piece is unique and beautiful.

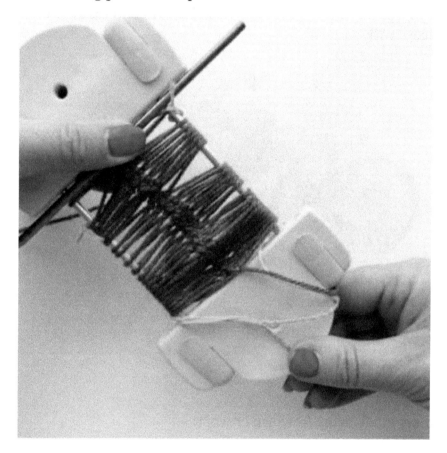

Items made using hairpin crochet:

- Delicate scarves
- Shawls
- Wraps

Micro Crochet

Micro crochet is a modern crochet style and is made using very fine yarn thread with extremely fine or small crochet hooks. It is a very delicate crocheting process and is great for those who are patient and like dainty and small things.

Item made using micro crochet:

- Tiny things for dollhouses
- Embellishments
- Talisman

Overlay Crochet

This technique is also unique where a base of crochet stitches is made, and then other stitches are added to the top to create a raised pattern. This crocheting technique is more advanced, and it brings many possibilities for you to create intricate pieces.

Items made using overlay crochet:

- Potholders
- Wall hangings
- Handbags

Pineapple Crochet

The pineapple crochet is considered more of a general stitch and shape rather than a technique. You can use this crochet to create scarves, doilies, and certain types of clothing. This stitch was very popular in the 1970s, and once you know how to spot this type of stitch, you will see it everywhere.

Items made using pineapple crochet:

- Dresses
- Tops
- Shawls
- Wraps

Stained Glass Crochet

The stained-glass crochet could be mistaken for the overlay crochet. However, it is different because the top part is normally made using only black yarn to accentuate the colors and create a stained-glass effect. What you get is a very striking crochet pattern.

Items made using stained glass crochet:

- Thick, sturdy items
- Winter scarves
- Handbags

Symbol Crochet

The symbol crochet is another type of popular crochet and is the favorite among the Japanese. It is also known as the "chart" crochet and is another one of those crochet skills that are crucial to learning because you can make any projects from any crochet books in any language and create them all by looking at a chart.

Items made using symbol crochet:

- Complicated patterns that are difficult to explain in words
- Intricate designs
- Motifs
- Foreign language patterns

Tapestry Crochet

As the name goes, plenty of color goes into creating this piece, and it is also known as "intarsia" crochet. Tapestry crochet is used in many different parts of the world, and it also has many different methods, which result in a variety of styles. If you want to do color work, using tapestry crochet enables you to create intricate patterns with a variety of colored yarn.

Items made using tapestry crochet:

- Color work pieces
- Imagery based designs

Tunisian Crochet

This type of crochet is done on a long hook that has a stopper at the end. When you look at Tunisian crochet, it can be very similar to knitting because of the many live loops, and you need to work your loops on and off your hook, similar to knitting.

Items made using tapestry crochet:

- Knit-look items
- Blankets
- Scarves

CHAPTER 5:

Essential Supplies for Your Crochet

Basics: You only need yarn/thread, crochet hooks and scissors to start crocheting.

Yarn

You can use a variety of yarns to crochet, but the type of yarn you chose depends on the type of project. You can crochet with any kind of yarn, even non-fiber yarn-like materials. While you can use any type of yarn, as a beginner, you will find it best to use the yarn options we will outline below since they are easier to work with than others are.

Choosing the Best Yarn for Crochet

Fiber type

This is the first decision you have to make as you embark on your crochet journey. There are quite a number of options to choose from for both plant and animal fibers. However, we will focus on the three most common and basic ones: acrylic, cotton and wool.

You might be wondering how to know which type of fiber you are working with, but it's really quite simple – the type of fiber is usually listed on the yarn label. Although as you familiarize yourself with crocheting, you will find yourself being able to identify the fiber type by just handling or even looking at the yarn.

Acrylic yarn: Acrylic is generally a popular yarn among crochet enthusiasts. It is usually among the affordable choices for yarn, comes in a variety of colors and is widely available. It is a more-than-acceptable choice for you as a beginner. However, you should be aware that some of the cheapest acrylics split apart, thereby making it quite challenging to work with. This case is not usually common, but it does happen. Therefore, if you are having a hard time working with acrylic, try switching to a different brand or you can just use wool or cotton instead.

Cotton yarn: It's an inelastic fiber, thereby making it a bit more challenging to work with than wool. However, where you want the item to hold its shape, this quality makes cotton a great choice for specific projects. Although some may find it a bit more challenging than wool, it is not that different at all, and it is something you can certainly try as a beginner. If you are crocheting during summer, where working with wool is unpleasant due to the heat, cotton is a great choice since it's lighter than wool.

Wool Yarn: Wool is the perfect choice for you to practice your stitches. It is forgiving of mistakes and is a resilient fiber. If you happen to make a mistake while crocheting, most wool yarns are easy to unravel and even re-use (in crochet, it's called frogging). Wool yarn is not suitable for those with wool allergies, but for most, it is a good crocheting choice.

Additional Yarn Tips and Considerations

Yarn weight: Yarns come in different thicknesses as well. This thickness is what we refer to as weight. The weight of the yarn is usually found on the label where it's numbered 1-7 (from the thinnest to the thickest). It is easiest to work with a worsted weight yarn as a beginner, which is #4 on the yarn label.

*Note: it is advisable that you use the correct crochet hook size for the yarn weight you will be using.

Yarn color: Choose lighter yarn colors rather than dark ones, as it can get challenging to see your stitches if using yarns with dark colors.

Yarn texture: Choose smooth yarn and not the textured ones. As you begin crocheting, avoid eyelash yarns and any other textured novelty yarns, which can get quite frustrating to work with.

Yarn yardage: Each ball of yarn has different yardage amounts, which relates to the price. You can find 2 balls of yarn with the same price; just check the yardage to ensure the amount of yarn in each ball is approximately the same.

Yarn price: The price of yarn varies significantly from brand to brand and fiber to fiber. It is better to work on the affordable ones so that you get the hang of it before investing a lot of money in very expensive yarns. This is why acrylic, wool and cotton are the top fiber choices, as they tend to be the most affordable.

Yarn color dye lot: If you want to crochet a large project that will need more than 1 ball of yarn, then you want to ensure that all the colors match (assuming that you are using the same color way or color for the entire project). You do this by checking the "dye lot on the yarn label to ensure that the balls are from the same dye lot number so that they don't have noticeable differences between them.

Washing details: Different fiber types have different washing instructions, which will be really important if you are crocheting something to wear. For instance, you can use superwash wool that is safe to put in the washer and dryer, or you can go for some type of wool that must be hand washed and dried flat because it will shrink in the dryer. The yarn label contains this information to aid in your selections.

Hooks

The average crochet hook works for anyone, and it definitely favors beginners like you. You will find crochet hooks sold at yarn stores or any major craft retailer. You can also get them online. Below are a few things you need to know about crochet hooks:

Material: A basic crochet hook can be made of several common materials such as bamboo, plastic and aluminum. Most people usually choose aluminum crochet hooks for their first project. There are also fancier crochet hooks made of wood, glass, and clay.

Size: Crochet hooks differ in size; there are many different sizes that are measured in numbers, letters or millimeters. For instance, a basic crochet hook set may range from E – J. A general-sized crochet hook is normally H-8 5mm. Size E is smaller than size H; size J is larger. As mentioned, you should match the size of your crochet hook with the weight of your yarn, which is usually on the label of the yarn. For most beginners, it is usually advisable to work with a size G or H crochet hook and worsted weight yarn. **Hook throat:** A crochet hook has either an inline or tapered "throat," resulting in less or more flatness to the head of the hook. Since neither is better than the other is, if you find it hard to work with one, just try the other.

Types of Crochet Hooks

Let us now look at the various types of crochet hooks at your disposal as you get started:

Thread Crochet Hooks

When you are using thread to crochet instead of yarn, the crochet hook you use is similar, but it is quite smaller than a yarn hook. The hooks are also usually made of steel in order to prevent bending while you crochet, a problem that is less popular among larger hook sizes.

Light-Up Crochet Hooks

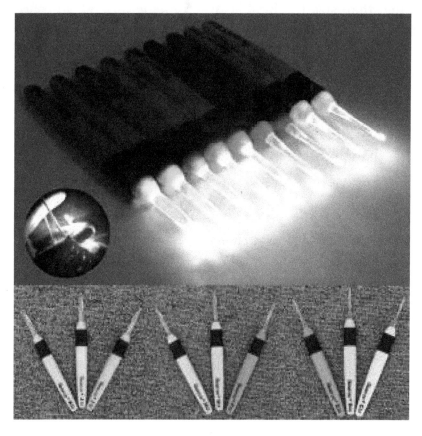

If you suffer from insomnia or if you simply want to crochet in the middle of the night without being a bother to anyone, then light-up crochet hooks are what you need.

They light up at the tip so that it is easier to see where you are going to insert the hook to crochet. They are typically regular crochet hooks that light up.

Ergonomic Crochet Hooks

Sometimes it can become quite uncomfortable to crochet with regular hooks for a long time, especially if you suffer from hand conditions such as arthritis or carpal tunnel. Fortunately, there are ergonomic crochet hooks, which have larger handles that are shaped to create a grip that makes it easier to crochet for long.

Tunisian Crochet Hooks

Tunisian crochet is a niche of crocheting that uses a completely different set of stitches from regular crocheting. Tunisian crochet hooks are also known as Afghan crochet hooks and are longer than regular crochet hooks. These hooks can have a cable to connect a one-headed hook to another one-headed hook, or they can have a head on either side of the hook.

Knock

A knock looks like a regular crochet hook, but it has a small hole drilled into one end where you insert the thread for holding your stitches.

Tools You Need for Crocheting

Crocheting is easy and fun! However, one needs the right equipment to complete a project successfully. The following tools are essential in crocheting projects:

Hook: This is used to make loops and interlock them into stitches. Hooks are composed of steel, plastic, aluminum, bone, tortoiseshell, or wood, among other materials. It is upon the individual to choose a comfortable hook. However, that choice is largely determined by the size of yarn and the holes that one wants, as well as the instructions specified in the pattern.

Hooks come in varying sizes, designs, and thicknesses. It is imperative to note that a larger hook would be used with thicker yarns, whereas a smaller hook is used with fine threads.

When first starting with crocheting, a good choice is to start with an I/9-5.50mm aluminum hook. It is very comfortable for beginners because it is light, and yarn grips to it very well while creating bigger stitches that are easier to see.

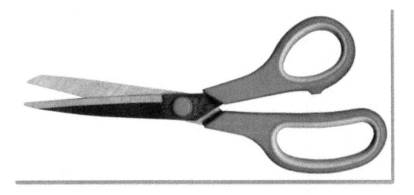

Scissors: They are used to cut the yarn after finishing a garment or sewing seams together. A small pair of blunt-end scissors in good condition is suitable for a crochet project.

Flexible tape measure: Used to measure the length and width of a garment to establish the gauge required by the pattern; a flexible tape measure is good for measuring both straight and round rows.

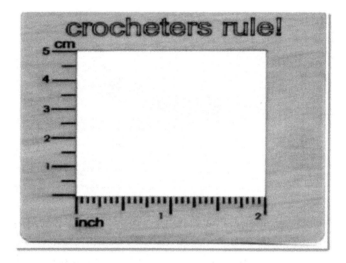

Gauge Ruler: This is a 2-inch L-shaped window item used to measure the number of rows and stitches in an inch.

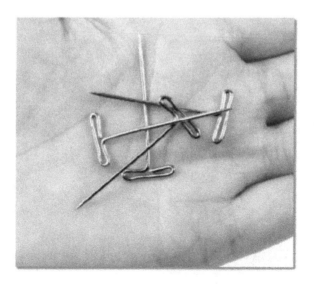

T pins: These are used to block and secure pieces of the project together when measuring, joining, or blocking.

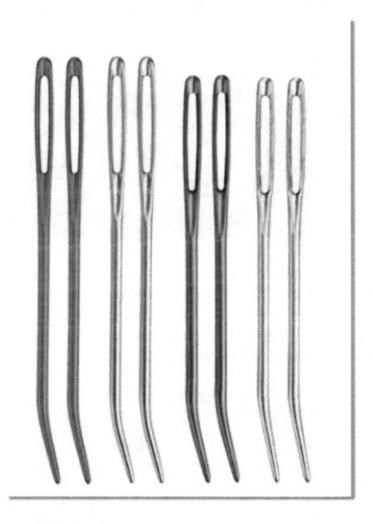

Darning/yarn/tapestry needle: This tool for hiding loose ends when joining yarn or seams of the completed project. The needle is made of plastic or metal and has a blunt point and a large eye. It can be straight or have a slight bend.

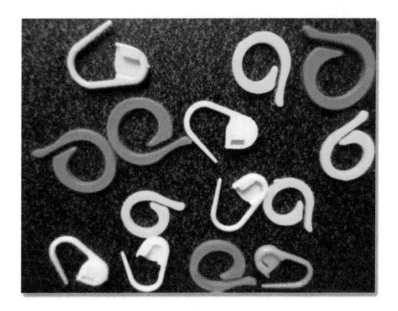

Stitch markers: These are devices that slip into a garment to show a certain point, such as joining continuous rounds, increase points or decrease points. They show where a stitch begins or ends, thereby keeping one on track. They come in different colors to make work easier.

Pencil and a small note pad: These are used to keep track of the row or round that one is crocheting or the number of times stitches have been repeated. They are also useful for writing small notes about each project.

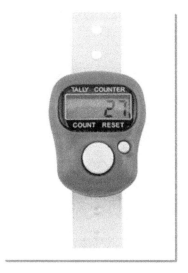

Digital row counter: This tool helps one keep track of crocheting work, such as the number of rounds made or rows completed, which in turn saves a lot of time.

Crochet tool organizer: This picture is an example of a useful crochet tool organizer that holds a hook organizer, scissors, and tape measures, among other crocheting equipment. You can make a crochet tool organizer or buy one from various shops.

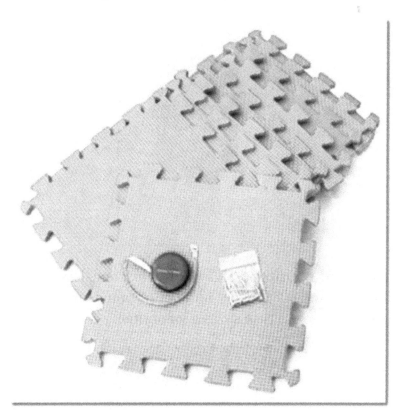

Blocking surface: Every crocheted needs a good surface for blocking crochet pieces. Any flat, soft surface such as a bed would suffice, but a more suitable blocking surface would be a board or a mat as pictured here.

CHAPTER 6:

Right-Hand Crocheting

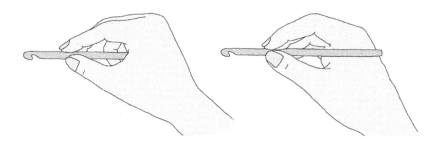

C rocheting, being one of the most famous home activities, for the right-handed crochets is more of the opposite of the entire aspects of left-handed crochet. Traditionally, this is one activity where our mummies or grannies practiced in early times. Due to the simplicity and reasons prompting people to indulge in crocheting, this activity is still practiced even today. Crocheting is a knitting technique for your materials like blankets, sweaters, or any other kind of dressing that is made by yarns. This activity is effortless and requires only the presence of thread and crochet hook. It also necessitates one to coordinate your working fingers and the string in a loop for this exercise. The work may involve single stitching and double stitching, which is basically dependent on the type of cloth you are knitting.

Considering the hand one usually uses very significant in this activity. Most people in this world are right-handers, and a low percentage is lefthanders. I am sure most of you have come across lefthanders, and you wonder how they operate their different tasks. Scientists believe that using the left hand is influenced by the right part of cerebral thinking. While using the right side is controlled by the left cerebral mentality.

Perhaps you may note some of the significant differences in using these hands. First, the right hands are a natural way of operating things. Its left part of the brain is mainly analytical, skillful, and verbally used; the right, therefore, majorly uses this part. The right part, which is used by the lefties, is mostly intuitive, where the person involved is mainly a creative and critical thinker. In any way, any dominant hand is stronger than the other. However, in embroidery, the right side is preferred because it needs analytical skills for successful crocheting. Building a pattern when sewing does not come easy; however, it requires your maximum concentration and coordination of brain with the fingers.

To perfectly crochet a cloth, one should first recognize how to obtain the right materials used for this activity. Having quality crocheting hooks and threads is essential in the provision of quality operation. The following are elements to consider in acquiring those items.

What to look for when searching for a good thread for the right-handed crochets:

As with any other crochet, the right-handed crochets must follow a series of steps in determining the best thread for their design. The first factor is to meditate on the outfits to sew. The style of crocheting for blankets is different from that of sweaters or any other clothing. Some garments require even triple stitching, while others are single crocheting. In that regard, think about how you want the garment to appear. There are certain materials like metallic threads or rayon floss, which are shiny and colorful, respectively. Therefore, they nourish the appearance of the outfit. What should be your priority is to produce a cloth that is attractive and pleasant to the wearers.

Before you start weaving your fabric, you should consider how to obtain a good thread. Some threads are standard and do not break easily, and they are also durable. Quality should be one of the factors to consider in choosing the right string. Cotton-based yarns are useful because they are simple to wash and do not tear off easily. They also do not fade quickly and retains their nourishment. Imagine how hurtful it would be when packing a bleeding strand together with your white shirt. Silky embroidery mostly shows such character. Therefore, when buying a thread, carefully consider the properties of its materials. The size of the fiber is also crucial for your crocheting plans. You should contemplate the fabric needed for the sweater or the cloth you are sewing. Even the number of apparels for your kids or family will constitute the thread to purchase. Determine how such items are sold to know the quantity you are capable of buying. Engage the sellers to instruct you on the size of the clothing a specific roll of yarn you can produce. Such measures will take help one in the budgeting concerns. Assess how the fabric is packed at the shop display. Most of the yarns are wrapped either in rolls, balls, skeins, or hank. All these arrangement styles improve their shows at the shop. At this time, you must be wondering why the strings are arranged in such patterns; that is because they have to be prevented from intertwining. When a thread tangle, it is hard to untie such knots, which would prove tedious when in a rush of knitting.

Assess the different types of thread to purchase; that requires extensive research to obtain knowledge of a product. There are many types of strings. However, with the practical knowledge of the design of your crochet, you are capable of choosing the best. Engage experts who recommend the best yarn in the market. Some of these yarns range from cotton or silky ones that the strings are relatively hard and do not cut easily. You may consider this when sewing hats or sweaters or tablecloths. Some are a form of embellishment in your dressing like variegated threads, tapestry yarn, and many others. Lastly, the hard pearl cotton is suitable for sewing blankets because of its hardcore stitching. Price is the predominant aspect that one must consider in buying any item. These threads come at different charging rates. It is upon you, the buyer, to investigate what the retailers offer in the market. Deliberate how those rolls of strings are sold; hence, buy from a relatively affordable store. However, do not trade quality items for cheaper rates as mostly substandard goods are the cheaper ones. Pricing thus should come after choosing the standard item you require.

To maintain your work very even, one should work the last triple crochet in that row up to the fourth chain of that turning chain of the end of the former row.

The Half Double Crochet

This is one type of lovely crochet stitch, and you should try to master it as it is so versatile. If you are comfortable with single crochet and double crochet, this should be a piece of cake.

It also comes as shorter than the double crochet stitch pattern. Choose the yarn you are going to use and crochet hook size that suits your work, there are so many you can use, and patterns will indicate what you need. If you are not using a pattern, just choose your yarn first, and the label will have information about which hook size you will need. As a beginner, you can try worsted weight yarn with a crochet hook of size H.

Follow these simple instructions in order to get the know-how of the half double:

Crochet Stitch

Crochet a chain as your foundation.

Work with the first half and insert it into the chain at the third chain stitch. Bear in mind that if you are crocheting in rows, start each row with the turning chain. For your half double crochet, work two for the turning chain.

Yarn over and then inserts your hook into the stitch. The yarn over is what gives it the height.

Yarn over once again, then pass it through the stitch. At this point, you will have three loops on your crochet hook now.

Again, yarn over, and then you pass it through all three of the loops this time.

Repeat these steps to create more half-double crochet stitches, crochet across your foundation chain, and then across all of the other stitches in the rows that follow.

To sum it all up for you, the half-double crochet goes as the following: The first step is to yarn over, then insert hook into the next stitch on the first chain, then repeat the same process again. Some useful half-double crochet information:

- It is quite common to replace the double stitch with a half-double stitch if you would prefer a shorter design that looks similar.
- If you are keen on crocheting blankets, you can make use of half double crochet stitches as they make the most beautiful edgings.

Turning Chains

These are chains at the very end of the row, which is made there to enable you to work from one row to the next while still being able to maintain the height of the row. The number of chain stitches in the turning chain differs depending on which stitch you are working in that row. It is one chain stitch for single crochet, for half double crochet, it is two, and double crochet stitches use three chain stitches in the turning chain. Rows worked in treble crochet generally use four chain stitches in their turning chain.

Some Other Points Worthy of Note in Crocheting

How to Hold the Hook When Crocheting?

It is very important that the hook is held properly while doing crochet work. This will reduce the incidence of pain in your wrist and will even make your work go on smoothly. They are the pencil hold and the knife hold.

The pencil holds

One way of gripping your hook is by holding it with your thumb, index finger, and middle finger. You can just imitate the way you will hold your writing pencil.

The Knife holds

You can also hold it like your knife, with your palm on the handle, your three fingers wrapped around it, and your index finger pointing towards the head of the hook.

In the real sense, we all have different ways of handling stuff. We all hold our writing pencils differently, and it is part of what accounts for the differences in handwriting.

Two different people might also have different ways of holding the knife. So, I will say find the style that suits you and crochet away!

Right and Wrong Sides of a Crochet Piece

In the art of crochet, working on the wrong side might lead the crocheter into making errors and therefore result in frogging. Working on the wrong side can also give a crochet result that is entirely different from what the crocheter had in mind.

RIGHT SIDE (RS)   WRONG SIDE (WS)

CHAPTER 7:

Left-Hand Crocheting

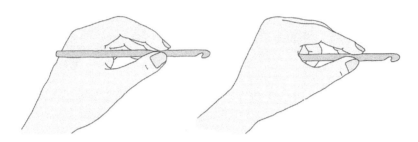

Being a left-handed crocheter is a unique thing because you will operate against the current status quo of things. This was due to the fact left-handed crocheters had to draw their knowledge from right-handed crocheters. Thinking about this is a little bit hard for left-handed crocheters. You can imagine learning a skill from an individual who does not have an understanding of it. Well, that's in the past.

Today, the situation is different, as left-handed crocheters have a vast number of sources from where they can draw their knowledge from. These sources include various tutorials, patterns, and teachers who have brought themselves to spread the mastery of this art.

When we talk about left-handed crocheting, this is almost as mimicking right-handed crocheting. This is because left-handed crocheting borrows a lot from right-handed crocheting. It can almost seem like a reflection of the other.

The left-handed crocheter, just as the name suggests, will hold his or her crochet on the left hand while the right-handed one will make sure that the crochet is on his or her right-hand side. There are various grips that one may assume when holding the hook. This includes the knife grip or the pencil grip. When this happens, the crocheter may manipulate the hook in whichever way he or she desires. With left-hander crochets, learning the basics and following the patterns of crocheting is subtle. This is because they are going out of their way in order to learn the mastery of what they have not been doing on a daily basis. Moreover, many crocheting patterns follow the direction of right-handed patterns.

In order to make this less subtle for you as a left-handed crocheter, you need to learn the basis of left-handed crocheting. Below are the various steps which can be very helpful when beginning left-handed crocheting or when maintaining its perfection.

The Hook Should Be in Your Left Hand

Crocheting left-handed will mean you will have to put the crochet in your left hand. This way, your right hand will have the leeway to support the work that you are manipulating. The hook has a flat part that is key when manipulating your work. When you are running the task, your thumb and finger should be on the grip of the flat part of the hook. Holding the crochet properly is key when it comes to effective sewing. The grip of the crochet should be maintained and balanced all through your sewing.

Chaining

The foundation of crocheting begins with this stage. When you are engaging in a crochet project for the first time, you will need to practice chaining. One of the less subtle techniques in crocheting is this one. In order to achieve this, you need to commence by making sure you loop the yarn on your finger. This is often done twice—your finger here meaning the index finger. After you have achieved this, the next step will be that you will gently pull your second loop through the first loop.

The result of this is what we call a slip-stitch. After this is achieved, you will need to make sure that you slide the loop that is on your hook with and loop it too. After this, you free the end of the yarn over the hook. In order to make another loop, you need to slide a novel yarn all the way through the loop that was already inexistent.

In order to make sure that the number of chains is increasing, you need to carry out this activity in a continuous manner. This way, you will find that you have achieved a chain. Forming a chain is the most basic stance of crocheting since you are carrying out this activity in a continuous manner. The chain should only be limited to the purposes of your project. When in demotion, chaining is often referred to by the abbreviation "ch."

Slip Stitching

A slip-stitch, as it is known, can also be referred to as a stitch that is jointed. The process of slip stitching is one that involves the insertion of the hook through the stitch. After this has been achieved, you will need to proceed to yarn over. In order to complete the formation of the slip-stitch, you will need to you need or make sure that the novel yarn passes through the stitch. With this at hand, you have accomplished the slip-stitch. With a slip-stitch, you can be able to move from one point to another. It can also be used as a link between two stitches. Linking two stitches is of key importance, for instance, when you are making a round while crocheting.

Single Crochet

This is a type of stitch which comes as a result of patterns. In order to achieve this type of stitch, you will first need to make sure that the hook goes through the stitch and then make sure that the yarn passes through both stitches. After you have accomplished this, you will need to make sure your yarn is over. This then involves the yarn being pulled through both the loops in a bid to hook it. When abbreviating a single stitch of crochet, this is often denoted as "SC."

Double Crochet

After you have achieved a single crochet, the next step will involve that you do a double crochet. These are other types of crochets that are also common. When double crocheting, you will need to yarn over twice in order to bring about the double effect. Yarning the second time will involve that you insert the hook through the stitch first before you a yarn.

After this has been achieved, you already have the first stitch. With this stitch in place, you need to pull through this stitch and then yarn. You have two stitches in place, and thus you can proceed to pull the hook through them and then yarning again. After pulling through the last two stitches, this will see to it that you get done with the stitch. When denoting double crochet, this is done by a denotation of "dc."

Half-Double Crochet

This type of stitch is not commonly known. Despite this, it is important we get to know this type of stitch. This is because when engaging in a type of work that is more complex in nature, you will need to employ the use of this particular type of stitch. In order to achieve this type of stitch, you need to yarn over, after which you then make sure that the hook goes into the stitch. After you have achieved this, you will need to yarn once more over this time; you are pulling through a number of stitches. It could be three. Half double crochet is often denoted as "hdc."

Triple Crochet

With knowledge of single and double crochet in mind, you will now need to focus on acquiring the knowledge of triple crochet. In order to achieve a triple crochet, your first move will be to yarn over twice. This way, you are in a position to make sure that the hook goes into the stitch and that you can yarn over once more. After you have achieved this, you will need to pull this yarn through the existing four loops. With this in place, you will further need to pull the hook over through two loops, after which you will then have to yarn once more. In order to finish the stitch, you will have to consider pulling through the final two loops. When denoting this type of stitch, you will do so in a manner that suggests the formation of a "tr."

Crocheting in a Circle

When carrying out this particular type of drill as left-handed, it will follow the same path as it would when you are right-handed. We have already gathered how to make a chain, which will be your first order of events. In order to crochet in a circle, you will first need to make a chain. You have already gathered how a slip-stitch works, and so after you have achieved a chin, you will need to gather it at the center by using a slip-stitch. When you have already achieved this, you are in a position to advance in your chain-making. Crocheting in the round is an effective way to make heavy scarves, cowls and hats.

Try Out Various Special Stitches

When crocheting, you can assume various different patterns that come in handy when you want to create something captivating. We have already had a feel of what basic stitches entail, and in order to comprehend more complex stitches, we will first need to have an understanding of the basic stitches. Apart from the basic stitches, we have already gathered, there exist other types of stitches that come in handy when creating something interesting. These types of stitches include pop-corn stitch, box stitch, and shell stitch. As a left-handed, there are a number of things that will stand out when seeking to put up with apt crocheting. Some of these factors include:

Left-Handed Tutorials

Crocheting is a practical venture. When indulging in crocheting for the first time, you will need to have as much practical assistance as possible. With reference pictures, you are in a position to effectively understand the formation of a particular type of stitch. This is because you are able to see it as it forms. Learning how to crochet is an uphill task, especially for left-handed individuals. The net is filled with a lot of tutorials that are on crocheting using the left hand. An individual may use this when seeking out crocheting. With a tutorial, you are blowing to follow through the whole process of crocheting all the way to your success.

This is because you can pause and rewind where you might not have captured correctly. Moreover, there are blogs of other left-handed crocheters that are in existence. Following them and acquiring knowledge from them is easier because they tend to relate to you. There are also left-handed crocheters books. These books are various in the market, and thus you can choose to settle on one that will work best for you.

Following the Pattern to the Letter

Left-handed crocheting entails that you encompass the same patterns that a right-handed crocheter would use. When you have a pattern for right-handed crocheters, you will follow the pattern to the letter only to use your left hand when doing this. This also means that you can use many right-handed tutorials to your advantage.

You may be watching a tutorial for right-handed crocheters, but when you follow through with your left hand, you will find that you achieve the same results. As a result, you find that right-hand crocheters and left-handed crocheters are one and the same. The only distinction is that one uses the right hand, whereas the other uses the help of his or her left hand.

Flipping Pictures and Images

Most left-handed individuals refrain from right-handed tutorials not because they cannot work for the benefit of them but because of their already formed perception about this kind of tutorial. In order to make sure this perception is eradicated from left-handed individuals, a left-handed individual ought to assume patterns and ways that will work to their advantage. One of the most tactful procedures a left-handed may adopt in a bid to secure a deeper comprehension of patterns is by taking them and inverting them. When you invert a picture that was taken by a right-handed individual, you will find that it appears as if it is from a left-handed individual. There are a number of points to note when dealing with left-handed crocheting. For instance, you need to leave your beginning yarning tail hanging. This should be done at the beginning of every project; its essence is deep-rooted to the instance that you should not crochet over it. The tails come in handy when creating a cue, whether you are on the right-hand side of the cue or the left-hand side.

The right side always manifests itself at the right bottom corner. Another point to note for left-handed crocheters is that every time you are adopting a position of yarning over, you are doing this in a clockwise manner. You need to master this move as this is what makes sense to the whole process of crocheting.

There are numerous patterns for left-handed crocheters; this may involve the written ones and also the visible ones that are visual. Although the visible ones seem easier, left-ended crocheting is possible for both types of crocheting.

This is because a crocheter is being asked to relay what is in the written or what is in the book to what he or she is actually engaging in. A pattern that has been written down can easily be followed through just by the use of cognitive awareness that for left-handed, the direction of the yarn will be a little different. There are various types of patterns, which, in order to work best, need to be reversed to be implemented with ease. For instance, there is a type of crochet pattern known as the tapestry pattern that requires reversing in order for it to work properly. There are also other patterns known as color work patterns that require a reversal in order for them to function properly.

When you reverse filet crochet, one that is used when writing words, you are in a position to read the letters that were written in a manner that is reversed. When a left-handed does not work on reversing this particular type of work, you will find that this creates confusion on the rows and the stitches.

Often, the expected outcome will not arrive because of the mismatch in the various rows and stitches. With symbol charts, this is directed to right-handed crochets. Owing to this fact, left-handed crocheters ought to follow the same drill as depicted in the symbol charts but in a manner that is opposing to the already depicted symbol.

This means that you will adopt the symbol but me an opposite manner. Reversing a pattern can be done in the consciousness of an individual. This entails the individual forming a picture in his or her head and in turn, reversing it. If you cannot do this, the best way to reverse the pattern would be by using a mirror.

CHAPTER 8:

Basic Crochet Stitches

Slip Stitch

The starting stitch to practice on is the slip stitch which is a look-alike of the single crochet stitch. It is necessary to connect the rounds, join squares, and edging to finish items off neatly. Get ready to try your first slip stitch.

Place a loop on your crochet hook, follow by slowly sticking the hook into the place where you want the slip stitch to be. Then simply hook the yarn around your needle.

Now you can pull the yarn through, and you can pull the new loop through after the active loop, which you already have on your hook.

Try this a few times, and before you know it, you'll be doing it in your sleep.

You have finished your first slip stitch. The slip stitch is useful for the following:

- Forming a crochet ring

Some patterns start by creating a ring in the center. Common examples are granny squares and hexagons. Patterns such as these often begin with a few chain stitches that you'll need to join to create a ring. The slip stitch is what joins the two ends.

It is simple to make a ring shape in crocheting. Stick in the crochet hook to the end of the chain and crochet a slip stitch.

- Join round with a slip stitch

Once you have completed around, there is likely to be a gap between the beginning and the end. The slip stitch is used to close the gap and join the rounds. It is commonly used when working granny squares.

If you are using a pattern, it will indicate whether or not you should do this. You may not need to work a slip stitch at all, particularly if your rounds are worked in a spiral.

- Slip stitches in surface crochet

It is possible to work a slip stitch on the surface of any crocheted fabric. Slip stitches are great for embellishing your crochet items. You can also use them to outline shapes and designs to give them a pop of color.

An easy way of doing this is to cut out a design, pin it on the surface and then work your slip stitch around it. You can mark the design effectively using this method. If you prefer, you can also use a fabric marker to draw the outline.

- Joining crocheted elements using a slip stitch

Slip stitches are suitable for joining crochet elements. For example, you can use this stitch to join your crocheted squares or even stitch up the seams on a pattern you are using. A slip stitch is usually suitable for joining any crocheted pieces. When joining two pieces together, insert your hook through both of them or along the edges as you work each slip stitch.

Chain Stitch

Following the slip stitch, this is usually the first stitch you'll create as part of a long chain. Chain stitches are an important foundation from which beautiful creations can be made. Crochet patterns often include chain stitches amongst the other stitches as part of the design. While you are practicing your chain stitch, focus on keeping your tension as consistent as you can and holding your crochet hook correctly.

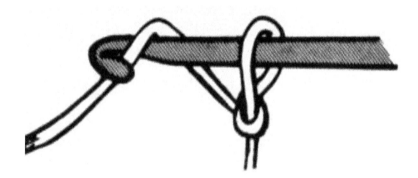

Take your hook with your right hand and hold it in the same manner that you would with a pencil or a knife, as long as you feel confident. As you begin, the hook should be facing upwards, and as you crochet each chain stitch, you'll need to your hook slightly in a counterclockwise direction.

Crocheting of the first Ch stitch: At this point, you place the hook inside of the slip knot you just made. You should loop the yarn steadily over your hook. This should be done from the back through to the front. To make this slightly easier, you can try holding your slip knot using the tip of your index finger.

As the crochet hook remains in the slip knot, all you have to do is a loop over the yarn from the back to the front. It may help by holding on to the slip knot on the hook with your index finger. Turn the crochet hook as you loop over the yarn to the hook.

Forming the First Chain Stitch: Once the yarn is hooked, pass it through the slip knot. Once you have pulled your yarn out, you can finish the stitch by turning the hook to its original position so that you can continue with the next one.

Onto the next chain stitch: So, you have made a chain stitch, and you can repeat this by hooking your yarn and drawing it through once more. Repeat this step over and over until your chain is complete.

Your index finger and thumb can be used to hold your chain stitches as you lengthen the chain.

In time, you'll be able to work rhythmically as you rotate the crochet hook so that you can hook the yarn and then draw it out once again.

Useful Tips for Making a Foundation Chain

- **Counting stitches:** As you count your chain, exclude the slip knot and start at the first chain stitch.
- **Do what works for you:** There are many positions in which you can hold your hook and yarn as you work. Try these according to the instructions, and feel free to change your position slightly if it makes it easier for you.
- **An even tension:** Keep practicing until you get your tension right and your stitches are not too loose or too tight.

Single Crochet (Single Crochet-US; Double Crochet-UK)

This stitch is vital as it is used in so many crochet patterns and is so easy to do. You can do so much with it. Whether you are working in rows, spirals, or rounds. It is also perfect for edging and combining other stitches. So, let's get to it, shall we?

Inserting the crochet hook: Once your chain is done, stick your hook in through your first Ch stitch. For the following row, you should put your hook into the single crochet stitch which lies beneath it in the row, and so on.

Slide your hook under both loops, which lie at the top of the chain. (Some patterns work through one loop at a time.)

The next step is to yarn over and grip the yarn: Draw a loop through and circle your yarn over your hook, and then pass it through with the hook.

You'll see 2 stitches that appear as loops.

Repeat yarn over: Circle the yarn around the hook as before, and then hook it.

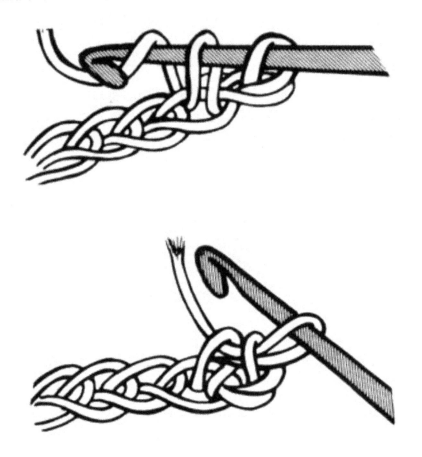

Pass the yarn through the two of the loops in one step.

Your single crochet stitch is done. As you finish, you'll have only one loop remaining, which serves as the insert for your next stitch.

To finish a row of single crochet stitches then all you have to do is simply repeat the steps as needed.

Just a hint: It can be difficult holding your work while stitching rows, the first row in particular. So, if it seems as if you are struggling, don't be discouraged; you'll get the hang of it. If you have someone who can do the first few rows for you, it will be easier for you to continue from there because it will be easier to hold it than a row which is still to be worked.

Once you are comfortable with the single crochet stitch, you can try doing the first few rows on your own. It will get easier, and you need to master this as you will need it in the future.

Variations of Single Crochet

You can change the look of a pattern by making simple variations of a single crochet stitch. Here are a few ideas.

Insert your hook so that it enters the front loop only (FLO) of the stitch on the top right-hand side. This is an open style of this stitch.

Insert your hook so that it enters the back loop only (BLO) of the stitch on the bottom left-hand side. This results in a stretchy ribbed look which is a rather popular variation.

Insert your hook through alternating loops (FLO, BLO, FLO, BLO) from the bottom right-hand side. You'll be able to create quite a textured look using this variation.

You may insert your hook in different positions, but your technique remains the same so that you can create simple variations of the single crochet. Using these will enable you to make beautiful, dense fabrics with which to create scarves and blankets if you so wish. These are useful items and canal be made using a single crochet stitch.

The Double Crochet (Double Crochet as Per the US; Treble Crochet as Per the UK)

The double crochet is another important basic stitch and is one of the foundational stitches, although it can easily be excluded from many simple patterns. You can use this stitch on its own by working rows or rounds, and it is popular in many common stitch patterns, such as the granny square, which is a classic, as well as the v-stitch. These instructions enable you to practice on your own until you are confident with using this stitch. One has to begin with one stitch on their hook, and then they should wrap the yarn over the hook of their needle. Next, insert your hook into the stitch. If you start with a foundation chain, stick your hook into your fourth stitch.

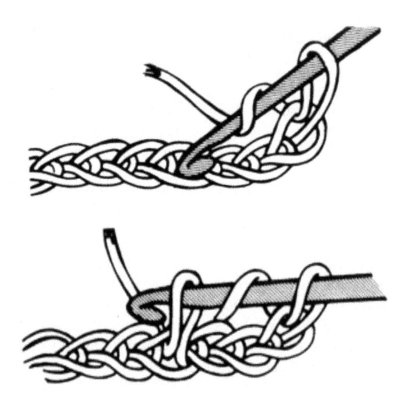

Then circle the yarn over the hook again so that your hook passes through the yarn.

You should circle your yarn over the same way that you did it when you inserted your hook the first time. However, now you'll have more yarn on the crochet hook, and it might seem slightly more difficult than it did earlier. It takes time to get it right.

There should be three loops left.

Repeat yarn over and draw it through.

Encircle the yarn over the hook once more and then pass it through the two loops nearest to the end of the hook.

Now there are some 2 loops on the hook.

Do the yarn over again and pull it through the loops that are remaining on your hook.

Now that you are left with only one loop, and your double crochet stitch is done.

You can build a rhythm as you practice this stitch so that you can yarn over and pass it through your loops; it will seem like one step.

Double crochet hint:

The easiest way to practice this stitch is by working it in a straight row. You can stick in the hook to the bottom of these two loops under your own stitch.

For patterns that include spaces, like the granny square, you can do the following: Insert your hook into space beneath the stitch you are working rather than into the loops. It is best to practice using regular rows and then go on learning how to work a double crochet into spaces.

You may have to work your double crochet into a different stitch. There are several variations of the double crochet. However, the basics of working double crochet stitches into rows will enable you to use any patterns.

Treble Crochet

This is yet another basic crochet stitch that you can easily master and is fairly similar to the double crochet stitch.

The difference between the two is that you must yarn over once more in the beginning so that you can create a slightly taller stitch than that of the double crochet. This is a great stitch, and you can use so many different types of yarns that can be worked in rounds or rows.

Treble Crochet Instructions

Start with a chain. To stitch your treble crochet in rows, you are going to crochet a series of simple chain stitches. Otherwise, you could also work your treble stitches directly into a fabric or any piece which you have started. In that case, you won't need to work a chain to start with; you can simply work your treble crochet into the next stitch.

The first four chain stitches on your chain are counted as the first treble stitch. For your next treble stitch, work to your fifth stitch from your hook.

To go onto your next treble stitch, encircle your yarn around your crochet hook twice. Now you'll see three loops on the hook, including your working loop, which was already there.

You have to yarn over the hook and draw it to pass through the two of the loops on your hook. At this point, you have two loops.

Again, you have to yarn over and then draw it through both loops on which completes one triple crochet.

To continue the row, then you should yarn over then follow by hooking twice, then stick your hook into the next chain and proceed to the triple crochet steps given before.

To make another row, make four chain stitches, then turn your work. This then is what counts as the first triple crochet in the following row, so you'll begin what is known as the triple crochet stitches in the 2nd stitch of the row that came before. To maintain your work very even, one should work the last triple crochet in that row up to the fourth chain of that turning chain of the end of the former row.

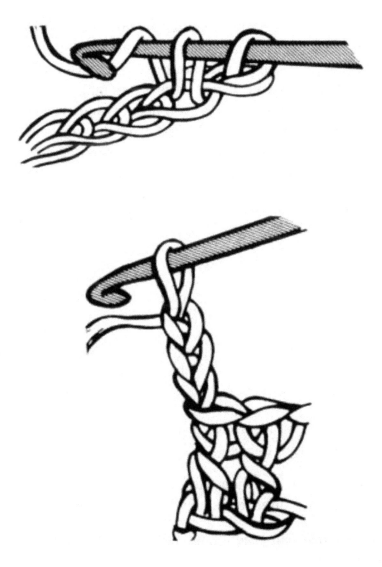

The Half Double Crochet (Half Double Crochet as Per the US; Half Treble Crochet as Per the UK)

This is one type of lovely crochet stitch, and you should try to master it as it is so versatile. If you are comfortable with single crochet and double crochet, this should be a piece of cake.

Half double crochet is taller than the single crochet stitch, as its name suggests. It also comes as shorter than the double crochet stitch pattern. Choose the yarn you are going to use and crochet hook size that suits your work, there are so many you can use, and patterns will indicate what you need. If you aren't using a pattern, just choose your yarn first, and the label will have information about which hook size you will need. As a beginner, you can try worsted weight yarn with a crochet hook of size H.

Follow these simple instructions in order to get the know-how of the half double Crochet stitch:

Crochet a chain as your foundation.

Work with the first half double crochet stitch and insert it into the chain at the third chain stitch.

Bear in mind that if you are crocheting in rows, start each row with the turning chain. For your half double crochet, work two for the turning chain.

Yarn over and then inserts your hook into the stitch. The yarn over is what gives it the height.

Yarn over once again, then pass it through the stitch. At this point, you'll have three loops on your crochet hook now.

Again, yarn over, and then you pass it through all three of the loops this time.

Your first part of the half double crochet stitch is done.

Repeat these steps to create more half-double crochet stitches, crochet across your foundation chain, and then across all of the other stitches in the rows that follow.

To sum it all up for you, the half-double crochet goes as the following: The first step is to yarn over, then insert hook into the next stitch on the first chain, then repeat the same process again.

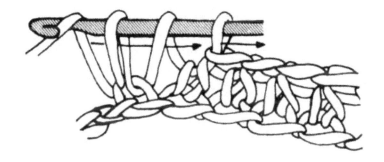

Some useful half-double crochet information:

- It is quite common to replace the double stitch with a half-double stitch if you'd prefer a shorter design that looks similar.
- If you are keen on crocheting blankets, you can make use of half double crochet stitches as they make the most beautiful edgings.

Turning Chains

These are chains at the very end of the row, which is made there to enable you to work from one row to the next while still being able to maintain the height of the row. The number of chain stitches in the turning chain differs depending on which stitch you are working in that row. For single crochet, it is one chain stitch; for half double crochet, it is two, and double crochet stitches use three chain stitches in the turning chain. Rows worked in treble crochet generally use four chain stitches in their turning chain.

CHAPTER 9:

Tips and Tricks

W hen you're new to something, everything might seem a tad overwhelming. Even if crocheting isn't a difficult hobby per se, this doesn't mean that it doesn't come with several challenges, especially during your first tryouts. Don't get discouraged, though, since we've all been there. What matters most is to keep going, and you'll realize that you're steadily making progress.

Turn Skeins into Balls of Yarn Before Starting Your Project

For one thing, you might feel impatient to get started with your very first crochet project. This might tempt you to rip the label off the skein of yarn and get started right away to see how things go. Nonetheless, even if you could crochet by using skeins of yarns, you might accomplish better results if you consider winding the skein into a ball first. As an expert, you won't tell the difference, but as a beginner, you will certainly see it.

If we were to compare balls of yarns with skeins, you should know they have several advantages. For one thing, they could help you avoid tangles. Usually, center-pull-skeins of yarn are prone to get tangled easily towards the end. On the other hand, balls of yarns don't tangle as much, which can really make a world of difference if you want to simplify your work.

In addition to that, if you find it difficult to accomplish to right tension when crocheting, you should work from a ball of yarn as opposed to working from a ball of the skein. To simplify this task, you could use ball winders—but you might also do it by hand.

Make Sure You Position the Yarn Correctly

It's always best to position the yarn correctly so that your project goes on smoothly. Basically, the ball of yarn should be positioned in such a way as to unwind easily as you crochet. Considering that you're crocheting at home from a comfortable chair, it might be a good idea to keep the ball on the floor by your feet or in your lap – depending on whichever option you prefer best.

On the other hand, if you're crocheting in a moving vehicle or in a plane, or any other place where you don't have a lot of space at your disposal, you should keep the ball inside a tote bag. This will prevent it from unwinding or rolling around.

When Needed, Change the Size of the Hook

Novice crochets have the tendency to stick to the hook they get started with. This must-do, of course, with convenience and comfort. Many times, the type of hook you start to crochet with gives you a certain degree of assurance, which is why the temptation to keep using it is high. This is common not only for crochet but for other types of handwork as well, such as knitting, embroidery, and the list could go on.

However, make sure you always consider the way in which your work evolves and make the necessary adjustments as you go. If you feel that your work seems too tight, you should simply switch the hook with a larger one. On the other hand, if you notice that the work appears a bit too loose, what you must do is choose a smaller crochet hook. Essentially, the hook size written on the yarn ball is merely a suggestion, and you shouldn't follow it blindly. As a rule of thumb, before starting a project—especially a complex one—it's best to give yourself time to do some experimenting.

Nevertheless, note that changing hooks in the middle of a project is contraindicated. That's because this will make your work appear inconsistent and uneven. And you don't want that. Even if you were to use the same size hooks from different manufacturers, you would still monitor several changes when you have a closer look at your project.

At the same time, depending on the type of hook you're using, this will impact the way in which you hold it and the way in which the stitching will look in the end.

Working on Your Tension: Why Is It So Important?

Working on your tension is important if you want to enhance your crocheting technique. In order to do this, you must keep the crochet in a way that feels comfortable—otherwise, enhancing your tension will be much more difficult. As we already pointed out, you should keep the crochet hook in the dominant hand—this depends on whether you are right-handed or left-handed.

Rest assured, as a beginner to crocheting, you are bound to hold the hook either too tightly or too loosely. And while practice will most likely contribute to solving these issues, there are also some ways in which you can do that, and we'll outline them in the following paragraphs.

Pull from the Center of the Yarn

This could be very helpful when you feel that your tension is too loose or too tight. For example, when you pull the strand from the outside, this will make the skein bounce all over the place, which will most likely be an impediment in attaining the right level of tension. On the other hand, if you focus your attention on pulling the strand right from the center, it will glide through your fingers more easily – which will allow you to feel better about your tension.

Have a Look at the Way in Which Experts Hold the Hook

Although copying the technique of an expert might not be the safest solution to this tension problem, it could help. Most likely, you can have a look at numerous tutorials online and see the way in which other people use their hooks. Once you do that, you can try it yourself and see what works best for you. Remember, there are no good or wrong ways to do this. The good thing is that there are many free online resources that could get you started when you feel clueless.

Since each person works differently, if you realize that what you're looking at is not your style, you should simply look at another technique until you find someone that works in a similar way as you do.

Choose a Beginner-Friendly Yarn

This is another useful tip if you feel that you're not making any progress. In fact, choosing a yarn that is difficult to work with might be an impediment, preventing you from making progress at a fast rate. On a different note, the tension you have when working with yarn will depend on the type of material you have chosen as well. For instance, as a beginner, your tension might be unsuitable if you're trying to work with cotton yarn, which poses some challenges to start with.

That isn't to say that all beginners will encounter difficulties when trying to work with cotton yarn, but some might. This is a subjective matter, and you shouldn't feel bad or anything – it's just that when it comes to crafts, every person has his/her own rhythm of learning and progressing. This means you shouldn't put too much pressure on yourself if things are moving a bit slower than you anticipated they would.

As a rule of thumb, when you're still trying to figure out how to attain the perfect level of tension, it's best to choose a material that has a bit of stretch to it. This will make your job easier. Over time, you can diversify the types of materials you're working with to ensure that you foster your skill and your creativity. But take your time.

In addition to that, we advise you to steer clear of novelty yarns or variegated yarns—particularly at the beginning of your crochet journey. These two types of yarns will make it especially hard to remain consistent in your stitches. Concurrently, these materials make it difficult to count the stitches, something that might be frustrating to beginners.

How to Avoid the Most Common Crochet Rookie Mistakes

Now that we've introduced some helpful tips on how to get better at crocheting let's focus a bit on the most common mistakes you are bound to make as a rookie. Knowing these in advance can be beneficial, in the sense that you might avoid making them altogether, which will allow you to save time!

- Crocheting in the front loop only

Novices to crocheting are bound to make this mistake. Therefore, we couldn't stress enough the importance of learning how to place the hook inside the stitch, as this represents the foundation of this handicraft. This mistake is likely to happen especially if the hook tends to slip from time to time and you don't realize this right away.

How do you avoid this common mistake? What you must do is simply have a closer look at the detailing of each row as you work. Basically, you should analyze each row. While this may seem tedious and time-consuming, if you practice enough, you'll get the hang of it, and you won't have to do it any longer. In time, your stitches will become second nature to you, so you won't have to stress about it.

- Your work seems to be getting wider and wider

This is likely to happen to anyone—beginners and advanced crocheting fans as well. Therefore, you shouldn't feel too discouraged if it seems to happen to you. This is bound to occur when you're not paying close attention to the stitches. On that note, one way to avoid this from happening is by counting your stitches—in this way, you will prevent ending up with more stitches than you had in mind when you first started working on this project.

You might be doubling up into one stitch, or, without your will, you might end up working a stitch in a turning chain. The safest and simplest way to prevent this from happening repeatedly is by counting your stitches. To that end, you might count each row as you finish or keep an eye on the shape of your project and determine whether it is developing as you had in mind.

You might feel that this is time-consuming, but believe us, it is more time-consuming to realize that you've been working for hours in a row to realize that you've made a mistake and you have to do the entire thing all over again.

- Not focusing on counting the rows while working

This mistake also has to do with maximizing your time. In the same way, in which it is advisable to count the stitches to the project you're doing, you should also count the rows to avoid unwanted mistakes. When you're crocheting, you can easily get distracted, as your mind tends to wander off, especially if you're watching a TV series or anything of the kind.

Staying focused is essential if you're just starting out, so make sure you are there, in the present, when working on your project. Otherwise, you'll realize that there are five extra rows of crochet, and you have lost your valuable time. You might resort to utilizing a row counter in case you end up making the same mistake repeatedly, as it will come in handy.

CHAPTER 10:

How to Choose a Crochet Pattern

Mussel Pattern

For this pattern, three or more stitches are crocheted into the same puncture site, forming a triangle that looks like a small shell. On the left and right of the shell, one usually goes over a few stitches to compensate for the increase in stitches by the shells, which turn one stitch into at least three. Shells look best if you crochet them out of chopsticks or double sticks.

In order to crochet a mussel out of three sticks, one works first, where the stitch is to be placed, first a stick, in order to work. Then in the same puncture, place two more sticks. To complete the pattern and the number of stitches in the row, it can sometimes be necessary to crochet half-shells at the beginning and end of the row. To do this, at the beginning of each turn, work two sticks into the corresponding puncture site. At the end of the row, place two sticks in the last stitch.

Tuft Stitches

Tufts are basically nothing but inverted shells. They consist of several stitched-together stitches; these can be fixed stitches but also double or multiple sticks. Not only do they provide a decorative pattern, but they are also often used to remove one or more stitches in a row.

The base of this tuft is spread over several stitches while their heads are gathered in a stitch. To do this, do not crochet the stitches you want to gather at first to pull the thread in one go through all loops on the needle in the last step. How to do it exactly shows the following instructions for a tuft of three sticks.

Work the first stick as usual until there are only two loops on the needle. Do the same with the second stick so that you have a total of three loops on the needle.

The third stick is also crocheted up to and including the penultimate step. There are four loops on the needle. Now, get the thread.

To complete the tufting, pull the thread through all four loops on the needle.

Burl

Knob stitches are very distinctive and give the crochet a beautiful plastic structure. It is a group of several rods or multiple rods, which are worked in the same puncture site and then blended together, making it a combination of shell and tufts. Pimples are worked in the back row. The following shows how to crochet a knot stitch out of five sticks.

Crochet the first stick at the point where you want to create the knit stitch until you have only two loops on the needle.

Follow the same procedure for the following four rods working in the same puncture site.

Now, there should be a total of six loops on the crochet hook.

In the last step, pick up the thread and pull it in one go through all the loops on the needle. It is advisable to secure the knit stitch with a chain stitch (take the thread and pull it once again through the stitch on the needle) so that the stitches remain firmly together at the top and the knobby effect maintains the desired plasticity.

Colorful Pimples

It looks happy when you work the pimples in different colors. In addition, you can meaningfully use small yarn remnants in this way.

To crochet a colored nub, work the last solid stitch in front of the nub in the base color until there are still two loops on the needle to finish the stitch with the yarn for the nub. Then crochet the nub as described in the new color. Use the chain stitch to secure the knob; work again in the basic color, with which you then continue crocheting until the next knob.

Flat Nubs

Flat knobs are made of half-sticks and are slightly less plastic than knobs or the popcorn stitches described below. They are often used to crochet baby clothes and cuddly blankets. They are crocheted according to the same principle as the pimples. It is important that you do not work too hard. The following example illustrates how to crochet a flat knot of three half rods in one go through all the loops on the needle. It is advisable to secure the knit stitch with a chain stitch (take the thread and pull it once again through the stitch on the needle) so that the stitches remain firmly together at the top, and the knobby effect maintains the desired plasticity.

First, thread the thread around the needle, then insert it into the loop into which the flat knot should be placed. Get the thread.

Repeat this step twice so that there are finally seven loops on the crochet hook. Then you pick the thread and pull it in one go through all the loops.

Finally, secure the flat knot with a warp stitch by retrieving the thread and pulling it through the loop on the crochet hook.

Popcorn Stitches

For a popcorn mesh, one works—as well as the knobs or flat knobs—a whole group of stitches in a puncture site. The stitches are not taken off together but individually terminated and bundled in a further step. They create plastic accents in even patterns and can be crocheted from fine yarn, as well as from thicker wool qualities.

Crochet a group of five rods in a single injection site when you wanted to crochet a shell. Then slightly lengthen the working loop on the needle by pulling lightly. Now, pull the needle out of the working loop in order to put it into the debarking element (i.e., the mesh V) of the first stick.

Then, pick up the working loop and pull it through the second loop on the needle (the debittering stick of the first stick). Secure the stitch with a chain stitch. Pull the thread through the loop again.

Filet or Net Pattern

For this effective but, in principle, quite simple pattern, you crochet from bars and air meshes a grid. You can combine filled and empty boxes in such a way that geometric or floral motifs are created. A simple net pattern without "fillings" can be crocheted very fast. For example, it is good for light scarves and bandages, and if you can handle it with sturdy material works, you would have crocheted, in no time, a shopping net. If you work alternately filled and empty boxes, you can pull a cord through the stitches to close about a bag.

Crochet a chain of meshes first. The number of stitches for your basic chain must be divisible by two. In addition, crochet six more pieces of air.

Now, for the first box, insert into the sixth stitch of the chain of stitches as seen from the needle and work a chopstick.

Crochet an airlock again. For the subsequent chopsticks, pass over a stitch in the sling chain. Then, crochet one more air mesh and the next chopstick into the next, but one mesh of the basic chain work. So, continue until the end of the series.

Start the next row with three first-streaks and one streak with the next-stick link.

Now, work a chopstick into the scraping member of the penultimate stick of the previous row, crochet a loop of air, pass one stitch of the previous row, and work another stick into the corresponding chopsticks of the previous row. The last stitch of the row works in the third link of the chain of meshes counted from below.

To crochet a filled box, do not join the sticks with an airlock, but crochet between the base stick's other sticks around the air mesh of the previous row. To do this, just stick in the empty box to get the thread.

If the box of the previous row is also filled, work the "stuffing stick" into the scraping member of the pre-row filler.

Grid Pattern

A likewise light and transparent pattern is the grid pattern, which is crocheted from air mesh and solid or warp stitches. Experimental minds vary the length of the air-chain chains to work an uneven lattice structure.

Normally, the arcs are one-third longer than the basic piece of the previous series. The arcs in the following instructions are five air mesh long, the base three chains.

Work an air chain. The number of stitches should be divisible by four. For this crochet, add two air meshes.

Now, anchor the first bow by crocheting it into the sixth stitch of the base with a slit stitch or a sturdy stitch. Then crochet five loops of air, pass three meshes in the basic loop and anchor the bow in the fourth loop of the air.

The last bow of the row is attached in the last loop of the base chain.

Now, crochet five air stitches and then a single crochet stitch into the bow, then another five stitches, and then a single crochet stitch into the next bow. The last bow is anchored in the third spiral of the first row.

Start the next series again with five air stitches, fasten them with a sturdy stitch in the first loop of air mesh, and work in the grid pattern to the end of the row.

The last tight stitch back into the third spiral air mesh of the front row work. Continue working until the desired height is reached.

Crochet Subjects Around an Air-Mesh Bow

In crochet instructions for flowers, for example, one often reads the instruction that a group of stitches, often chopsticks, should be worked into an air-mesh arch. For this, you do not sting into the mesh links of the chain but into the bow so that the chain of mesh is crocheted.

CHAPTER 11:

Easy and Fun Patterns for Beginners

A crochet pattern could make a perfect, beautiful handbag with fashion colors that you can modify over the seasons.

Patterns can come in different sizes and shapes, depending on exactly what you want them to be used for. The crochet designs often take the shape of animals or flags. Even the most patriotic of us colors can be matched to the desired effect with the yarn.

There are so many crochet patterns out there in magazines and the internet. There are thousands of templates, but you will find great original patterns no one else has by using your own imagination. It is not just women who can take advantage of crochet patterns; there are also designs for children's clothing and designs for men.

Men may use patterns on jacket arms or launch a new trend, for example, on bike jackets and bowling shirts. Vintage designs are available for women in the colder months in the form of scarves, capes, and coats for individual fashions.

Creating a crochet pattern can be very easy if you know the basic crocheting and different pattern stitches. Then you just need the yarn and the right size hook to complete the item for the design you want to display.

It may be a good idea to draw it on paper first to create your own crochet pattern. When the layout is complete, the template can be used for guidance on the ideal yarn and color in a local yarn shop. Make sure you have the correct yarn weight because it will decide whether or not the item is expandable.

When you are new to crocheting, before making your own, it is worth trying some patterns; get a feeling for the thickness and weight of the yarn before you move into advanced designs, and make patterns for yourself.

The most successful way to learn pattern techniques is through books that can be found at reasonable prices and sometimes even free on the internet! Some articles demonstrate the patterns and stitches involved and how to do that so everyone can practice a bit.

For charity shops and in shopping centers, there are so many trends. Specialty shops typically have a large product range. Seek to reach the shop and pick a fabric to feel the weight and texture before you buy the design. It will help you get home and start crocheting.

Crochet designs don't always have to be brand new; retro patterns have recently returned to the style and can be used in summer with lighter yarn and color for each season, and don't forget darker and heavier yarns during winter. Who should say when and how do you wear your crocheted items?

The world of crochet has changed, and with new designs and yarns, you can actually make unique and individual pieces.

Why not take a look at the 15 basic and easy-to-use crochet patterns below:

1. Crochet Wristbands

Crochet wristbands are so cheap and fast to whip up that they are the perfect complement for young girls and adults. This pattern is very easy to crochet to any size you like, making it easy in any material to crochet. The crochet wristband is designed to slip over the wrist so that the loop is removed. And most kids will be healthy and safe.

Materials

- ✓ **Yarn:** Red Heart Super Saver #4 or a size of 3 or 10 Crochet.
- ✓ **Theme Hook:** H/8-5.00 mm for #4, A G for 3, and a 1, 65 mm for 10.

The skill level for this pattern is Easy / Intermediate.

The finished proportions are the following: they measure roughly 3.5" in dimension. They can, however, be modified to any size if appropriate.

This design demonstrates how to everything in one color of the bracelet. So, it's simple to add a little more color in the second round by shifting to a new color.

Instructions

In Weight Yarn and H Hook:

1) Loosely Chain 22 or any number.
2) Incorporate a slip stitch in the first line so that the chains don't twist.

Round 1: Chain 1, work in the rear bumps and in each chain around; put in the first single crochet a single crochet slip stitch. (22 points.)

Round 2: Chain 1 (single crochet, triple crochet) in the same stitch as a join, * skip next loop (single crochet, triple crochet).

Repeat from* around; add a slip in the first crochet single. (22 stitches)

Round 3: chain 1, single crochet stitch in and around each thread, slip thread in the first single crochet. (22 sts).

Fasting off

Inside a size 3 Thread and a G Crochet Hook: chain 30, obey the instructions above.

In Size 10 Thread and a 1.65 mm hook in steel: chain 56, obey the instructions above.

In order to crochet this wristband to a customized scale, simply increase or decrease your stitches in several of two.

2. Crochet Scarf Making Use of Moss Stitch

This pattern is fairly simple for beginners. It does not need an increase or decrease as long as you are aware of how to work a single crochet and chain stitch; this scarf can be completed.

That said, for anyone interested in a soothing project, it is a great crochet design, so do not be afraid to bookmark it to a basic crochet scarf pattern though you are an expert crocheter.

Materials

- ✓ **Weight yarn:** This scarf can be used with worsted weight yarn. Select your favorite.
- ✓ **Crochet hook:** size K. (Of course, you may also use yarn with another weight, but that can greatly alter the finished size of your crochet scarf.)

Note: the hook can be changed to gage. Nevertheless, if you are not chic about the finished size of your scarf, the gage is not too significant.

- ✓ **Tapestry needle:** You are going to have to thread this in the ends when the scarf is done.
- ✓ **Stitch Marker:** you will need a stitch marker to mark a stitch temporarily. This is done to make the first-row job easier. You do not need anything fancy.

Following the calculation below, you create a narrow hook scarf that is about 4 inches long. It is simple to adjust the length of your crochet scarf, depending on the number of rows in your crochet. It produces a thin scarf long enough to surround an adult. Make it short for a simple child's crochet sharp pattern, with fewer rows.

To test your stitch rate, crochet 10 to 12 rows of the pattern and weigh the scarf width. Compare this measurement with a 4-inch measurement. If your scarf is wider than this, you may want to start with a smaller crochet hook. In comparison, because it is smaller, a wider crochet hook may be used.

Crochet scarves are made in several different widths, so it is nice to make them as smaller or wider as 4 "on average. If the scarf looks as though it would be wearable in the width you produced it, there is no need to start again unless you purchased a large amount of yarn.

- ✓ **Row Gauge:** the row gauge is not necessary for this particular pattern since the length of the scarf depends on the number of lines in your crochet. You can crochet as many rows as you want to achieve the perfect scarf length.

Crochet scarf style states the brackets '[]' suggest a series of repeated instructions.

If you have trouble locating your ch-1 spaces, continue to trace your finger carefully from rear to front, feeling your way to the job as you hang up to see where these spaces reside. In each row, you end up with a minimum of 7 ft.

Instructions

Free Scarf Pattern for Crochet Ch 15:

Row 1: Place a stitch marker in your hook's first ch. Sc in hook 3rd ch. [Ch 1, skip next ch, sc at next ch] Bracket sequence] [5 more times in a row. Ch 1, transform. Ch 1, transform. Here you should have your first set of 7 sc across the board.

Row 2: [Sc in the following ch-1 sp, ch 1.] Rep sequence in brackets] [5 times in a row. At the end of the row, work the marker in a single crochet st, remove the marker prior to working the stitch. Ch 1, transform. Ch 1, transform.

Row 3 and up: The remaining rows are similar to row 2, but with a small difference: at the end of the row, you are going to work your last sc st in the last row. That is how you crochet the mother's thread. Rep this row until the scarf is as long as the scarf is.

End the Crochet Scarf

Fill in the tapestry needle and thread it into the work so that it cannot be seen. Repeat for any other loose ends that you might keep. That's it; put around your neck your crochet sharp and enjoy using it.

3. Crochet Washcloth

This pattern is as basic as possible and, you can finish with a useful cotton dish or washcloth. You can use any worsted weight yarn (it says the size on the label) you like. I read that many people are using acrylic for dish scrubbing.

Materials

Any Worsted weight yarn pattern is equipped with:

✓ Cotton Lily Sugar N Cream in Batik, White, or Gray (select any colored color you want).

Instructions

Scissor Pattern:

Chain 19*Single Crochet in the second chain from the ring. Single crochet in each row stitch.

Turn * Repeat the desired width of * to * at the bottom of the row chain, cut yarn, tie off and weave at the end with your wallpaper needle. Very fast! And note, the best thing is that if this does not prove to be ideal, you can still use it.

Washcloth Set Crochet Pattern:

Worsted Chosen Yarn Type:

Cotton Suggested Yarn:

Cotton: Dusty Rose colors and Navy Yarn Yardage:

65 yds Tools – Scarves, Approx. tapestry needle.

Finished dimension: 9.5 "by 9.5" Size: 2 "= 5.5 single crochet

Pattern details:

The given colors were used in a sample to produce 2 chocolates Ch 26.

Row 1: Sc in the second hook ch and in each st in...

Row 2: Ch 1, turn. Sc in every st in...

Row 3: ch 1, transform. Sc on the first 2 sts each.

* Sc on next m, dc on next m; repeat from * around.

Row 4: Ch 1, switching to the last 3 sts. Sc into the first pt.

* Sc in the next pt., dc into the next pt. Sc to the last 2 meters.

Section 5-29: Rows 3 and 4 30-31 repeat: section 1, switch.

Cut the yarn in every st and tie it off, tissue in every end.

4. Crochet Hand Towel

Materials

- ✓ Five colored yarn skeins, crochet thread, needle, and pin.
- ✓ Two 50 g knit picks ball cotlin dk yarn swan / naturally One 50 g knit picks cotlin / navy one 50 g knit picks cotlin / teal
- ✓ One 50 g ball knit picks cotlin / red Moroccan red / red tapestry one-inch needle with large hole.
- ✓ Any DK tapestry hooks cotlin / navy

Since you only need a small amount of the second natural-colored yarn ball, you should have enough to make two towels if you buy three balls.

Gauge 12 stitches and 14 rows = 4 cm / 10 cm working pattern (single crochet and pique stitch line).

Finished scale About 10 1/2 cm by 18 inches (26.5 cm by 46 cm) plus hanging loop.

Instructions

Before you start making the towel, you should know how to make the pique stitch. This stitch can be learned easily and produces a good texture.

Yarn over and bring the hook from the crochet or the first stitch of the row into the 3rd ch.

Draw a Loop Blue crochet hook drawing a white stitch yarn thread.

Yarn over and make a loop. Three loops will be on the hook.

By now, the stitch looks like double crochet, but the next step is a bit different.

Draw a Blue crochet hook through two loops, drawing a loop through two loops.

Yarn over and pull it over two chains. Two loops will be on the line.

Draw a loop through the crochet hook in the same stitch, make over a yarn and create a loop in the same pattern.

File over and insert the hook into the ch or stitch, as you also did at the start. Draw a circle. Draw a circle. You will be on the hook with four loops.

Yarn for another time and draw all four loops. You will have a hook loop.

Create the hand towel with a pique pin blue crochet hook making a four-pattern pattern.

It is now time to use the picking stitch when you crochet a striped towel.

5. Face Scrubbie

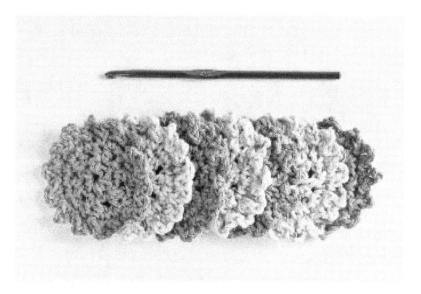

Materials

- ✓ Worsted weight of cotton yarn (around 8 yards)
- ✓ Crochet size H/8 (5 mm)
- ✓ Yarn or tapestry needle (Gauge does not matter for this pattern).

Instructions

Teal yarn crocheted into a circle of a violet hook Ch 4 and sl st to form a ring.

Round 1: ch 2 and then sc in the center. [CH 1 sc in the middle] Repeat this 4 times. Ch 2 and add sl st to the first stitch. 12 stitches will be around the loop.

Round 2: Approximately 2: ch 2. [hdc in the last round gap 2 times, ch 1] Repeat 5 times. Hdc into the preceding round void. Ch 1 follows the first stitch with sl st. 18 stitches will be around the loop.

Round 3: ch 2. [sc 2, ch 1] repeat this eight times. Sc 2. Sc 2. Join the first stitch of sl st. The circle will contain 27 stitches.

Round 4: ch 1. Ch 1. [Ch 3 and sl st in next sc.] Repeat twelve times. Ch 3 and in the last stitch sl st.

Secure the last stitch with a yarn or tapestry needle at the foot.

These little rounds of work are quick and are fun to work on. It is also a perfect way to use the skeletal ends after cutting dishcloths. Make a bunch of them, and you have got a lot on hand.

When removing your makeup, use your finished scrubbies as mini washcloths to purify your face in the morning or in lieu of disposable cotton rounds.

Pick the scrubbies used in a mesh washbasin bag and throw them into the wash.

They are also a fantastic gift. Print them all in a single color or crochet them in a rainbow.

6. A Crochet Heart

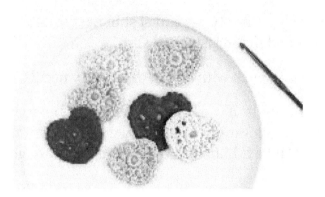

Materials

From 4 to 5 yards of yarn:

- ✓ The Crochet hook is not essential to this pattern in size, matching your yarn or wallpaper needles.

Instructions

Start the crochet heart by making a magic ring.

Make a knot slip and then ch 4 and form a ring sl st.

Change your jobs so that the back of your job is the slip knot.

Round 1: Work SC Stitches Crochet Heart

SC Stitches ch 1 for rotational chain and then sc 10 times into the middle of the ring.

Join the slip stitch with sl st when you shaped the loop. You normally will join the turning chain; it helps to shape the heart indent by adjusting the location of the joint. The circle will be 11 stitches.

Round 2: DC work and HDC crochet stitches round 2-DC and HDC stitches Skip the turning chain and continue your first double crochet in the first one.

2 times [dc, ch 1]. 2 times [hdc, ch 1].

Dc, ch 1. Ch 1.2 times [hdc, ch 1]. 2 times [dc, ch 1].

In the last two stitches, sl st. There will be 19 stitches around the perimeter, now more like a heart.

Round 3: Work SC Crochet Stitches Round 3-SC Stitches ch 1 for rotation line.

[1] 8 times. Fasten the single crochets on round two instead of the breaks in the chain stitches. Sc 2 in front of the dc line. Ch1. 9 times [sc, ch 1]. Last stitch sl st.

Complete the Crochet Heart.

Weave at the end of the yarn.

Cut the yarn and leave it about six inches. Secure the final stitch and wave with a yarn or tapestry needle in the ends.

When you secure the yarn at the corner of the neck, thread it towards the corner, helping to complete the neck form.

Finished Crochet Heart.

You would definitely want to do far more when you make a crocheted heart! What will all these hearts do? Here are a couple of ideas:

Make a heart garland by linking the hearts on a chain stage. Pass your hook through the back of a heart when you make the chain, and then add more chains and more hearts.

Craft-friendly heart pins and family sets.

Just thread a pin back into the heart. Maybe you want to first add a felt backup.

Develop heart cookies crocheted to make the faithful play. Create a heart on a bigger hook (or add an extra round of single crochet) with tan yarn to create a little larger one.

Then make the frosting a second heart. Stitch them with fun "sprinkles!" thread! Stack together a bunch of bigger crochet hearts and tie the pile to a ribbon. Now you have the perfect coaster or washcloth set!

7. Crochet Baby Blanket Pattern

This crochet blanket design contains instructions for three sizes: preemie, pregnant and baby children. Instructions list the smallest size with changes in parenthesis for larger sizes first. The following steps have no edges; if you want to add a baby blanket edge, the finished blanket will be a little bigger.

Materials

Preemie: The smallest blanket is about 26 cm wide and 34 cm long. To complete this project, you will need 2 to 3 5 oz skeins of yarn when you crochet your blanket using Bernat Softee. As far as yardage is concerned, the blanket itself takes about 724 yard / 662 meter plus a little more for your swatch.

Blanket newborn / receiving: a blanket of medium size is 30 inches long. You can make it a little longer if you want to make the blanket more rectangular. If so, try 30 "x 34." Depending on how close you crochet, you need two to three of Bernat Softee's 5-oz balls for this scale.

Toddler: 36 inches by 44 inches is the largest blanket. Four 5-oz Bernat Softee balls are required to crochet this amount.

Additional Crochet Materials

- ✓ **Crochet Hook size I**. (You may need a different size hook to get the right size).

Use this tapestry needle when you finish crocheting your blanket.

- ✓ **Marker:** Use a stitch marker or safety pin to mark a stitch at the start of your work.
- ✓ **Gauge Stitch gauge:** 4 stitches = 1 inch when the stitch pattern is crocheted as described below.
- ✓ **Row gage:** for this design, row gauge is not significant.

To check your size, make a size swatch. Crochet a size swatch. Shape a 25-stitch starting chain with blanket pattern instructions until the piece is square. Start off. Finish off.

Measure your swatch to see how many stitches you crochet per inch. Compare your gage with the one in the template (above). Use a smaller crochet hook again when you crochet fewer stitches per inch than suggested.

You need to swatch since you want your baby blanket to be a functional size. Unless your gage is different, your cot may end up in the wrong size, or you may run out of yarn before the blanket is done.

The design directions tell you to crochet the ch-1 spaces. If you find it difficult—sometimes they seem to disappear—push your finger carefully from the back to the front in a row of stitches. Your hands sense the distance, but your eyes do not first note it.

Instructions

Note, the instructions are small (in the parenthesis).

Row 1: Put the stitch marker in your hook's first ch. Sc from the hook in the 3rd line. [ch 1, skip next ch, sc next ch.] Rep all over the lines. Ch 1, transform.

Row 2: [sc in the next ch-1 sp, ch 1.] Replace the brackets sequence in the remainder of the row. At the end of the row, work an sc st in the st where you put the marker; the marker can be removed before the stitch is processed. Ch 1, transform.

Rows 3 and Up: All the remaining rows are the same as Row 2, with one small difference: move the last sc st at the end of the row through the previous row's turning chains. Rep this row until the baby blanket reaches the length you want.

Note: If you choose to change to a new yarn ball, use the same procedure as you would for color change.

When the baby blanket is as long as you want, cut off your yarn, leaving a total of six inches of extra yarn. Tread the tapestry needle with the end of the yarn and thread the loose end of the yarn into the blanket with the needle. Repeat for any other loose end (which happens when you turn from one yarn ball to the next).

This pattern works fine without additional edges, but if you want, you can add an edge. Many baby blankets are to be selected. A single crochet stitch around the entire edge of the blanket is a simple option that goes well with the individual crochet pattern.

8. Crochet Infinity Scarf

Materials

Any DK weight yarn will work for this project, however. You can also use worn-out weight yarn for a finished scarf that is a little bigger. If in warmer months you make bright wear, you might try cotton yarn.

Crochet Hook Using an I-9 hook size or any hook, you need to get the right gauge.

You would need to thread a tapestry needle in the finished size. The finished scarf measures about 61 inches. When putting flat on top of each other, it is about 30.5 inches. It is around 7.5 centimeters long. 19 points = 5 inches. This decrease to just fewer than 4 stitches per inch.

In this pattern, Stitch Gauge is important; Row Gauge is not as critical to success.

Design Notes

Several different sizes fit well for this particular scarf type. This site is a decent fundamental scarf but functions as a smaller and larger scarf.

Please take into account your personal preferences when assessing your work and testing your gauge.

The two key considerations are to achieve the size that you will be satisfied with and, at the same time, to create a bigger scarf, to not run out of yarn.

If you want the scarf to be longer so that you can create more loops, start with a longer beginning chain. You can also shorten the scarf with a shorter starting thread. The starting chain will have a number of stitches divisible by 6 and 4 in order to allow such changes. For instance, 216 chains work, and 240 chains work.

Instructions

Running the Infinity Crochet Scarf Pattern Ch 228, please note that this amount will vary if you want a shorter / longer scarf.

Sl st, touch the end of the chain to beg, holding the chain straight. Do not let it twist.

Round 1: ch 1. Job 1 sc in a ch for a total of 228 sc. Sl st to join the research in the round for the first st.

Round 2: ch 3. It is the first dc in the ring. Dc in next st, [ch2, skip next 2 hp, and function 1 fM next to 2 fM.] replaces it with brackets in the entire series. Sl st to join the beg at the end of the line. You will finish with 114 ft. in the round and 57 ch-2 spaces.

Round 3: ch 1. Job sc throughout 2 sc ea ch-2 sp. Sl st and function 1 sc ea dc to be able to join the beg at the end of the line. A total of 228 sc in the round will end.

Round 4: ch 3. The number is 1 hdc plus 1 ch a and Skip next st, [hdc in next st, ch 1.] Skip the series all-round in brackets. Sl st to begin the job in the round with the second ch st. A total of 114 hdc sts in the round and 114 ch-1 spaces will end.

Round 5: ch-2 sp sl st next, ch 3. The number is 1 hdc and 1 ch. [hdc in next ch-1 sp, ch 1.] Rep series in brackets. Sl st to be replaced in the round to the second ch st.

Round 6 – Round 14: Rep round 5. This is the easiest place to do so if you want to change the height of your scarf; out of one or more of these rows for a skinnier scarf.

For a large scarf, swap 5 more times.

Round 15: next ch-2 sp sl st. Then function sc as follows: ch 1, [Sc in ch-1 sp, sc in next hdc.] Replace the sequence in all sections of the brackets.

Round 16: Rep about 2. Round 2.

Round 17: 3rd round.

Edging Finished.

Crochet Infinity Scarf Shell Stitch:

Start with your active crochet needle. [Skip the next two sts. [Skip next. Function the shell in the next st like dc, ch 1, dc, ch 1, dc, ch 1, dc, ch 1, dc, ch 1, dc. Then miss the following 2 chs. Sl st in next st.] Rep the chain all the way around in brackets. You will finish with a minimum of 38 crochet shells.

Next Round:

When the shell sts are done, work around with a pair of crochet surface slippers. When you first work this round, work the surface of the crochet where the last round, round 17, meets the shell's rim. Work this round on the other side, where round 1 hits the edges of the container.

Replace these two border rounds around the free bands of your starting row. You will need to build an active loop to get your research started.

You can do so in various ways. Seek to insert the hook into one of the free loops in the start chain and pull up a thread, leaving an additional long tail of the yarn.

Terminate Off Weave at all loose ends. If desired, block.

9. Free Crochet Headband

Materials

- ✓ **Products Yarn:** worsted wool yarn 60 yards / 28 gr. The comparison uses Swish Worsted Knit Picks in Conch.
- ✓ **Crochet hook:** Scale I/9 – crochet hook 5, 50 mm (adjust to get the correct gage).
- ✓ **Other:** needle tapestry to weave in ends.

The completed headband measures about 19 "in diameter. At its narrowest point in front, it measures about 2-1/4 inches high and 3-1/2inches long at the highest point in the back. You may change the diameter at the end of each segment by adding or removing a row.

Measure the job after the first 5 rows of the pattern. You need a square of around 2-1/4 inches long. Consider using a small crochet hook if it is larger. Use a large crochet hook if it is smaller.

Stitch Variation: This headband pattern uses a half double stitch variation in which you are operating only in the back loops of the stitches.

Style Notes

Ch 2 for the turning chain between each board; the turning chain is 1 hdc st in all.

This headband begins in the middle of the piece and works backward; you then rotate the work and crochet the mirror image of the first half of the piece.

By breaking the yarn and beginning in the middle, you can stop weaving in extra ends. Pull approximately 30 meters of yarn and wind it in a ball, then start to crochet. You can use them later with some free scrap yarn patterns if you finish up with yarn leftovers.

Instructions

Divide the yarn and make the starting slip knots—a job with the little ball yarn ch 10.

Row 1: hdc in the third ch of the hook and every ch over. The first two chs in the row are the first hdc st, which gives you 9 hdc sts in total.

Rows 2–6: Work hdc over blo for each st. In each row, you will have a total of 9 m.

Row 7: Work the hdc over the block in each st. Take 2 hdc sts to the turning chain at the end of this line for a total of 10 m in a row.

Row 8: In through st, function hdc via blo = 10 m in a row.

Row 9: Work 2 hdc sts into turning chain for 11 sts at the end of row.

Line 10: Job hdc in through st by blo. Total = 11 m in line.

Row 11: Work 2 sts hdc in turning chain at row end for a total of 12 sts in row.

Row 12: In through st, work hdc via blo = 12 sts in row.

Row 13: Work half a double crochet column—work 2 hdc sts for a total of 13 mts in the row into the turning chain.

Row 14: Function hdc in through st through the blood = 13 meters in a row.

Row 15: Work 2 hdc sts on turning chain at the row end for a 14 m in a row.

Rows 16–20: Work hdc in each st by block = 14 m in each row.

You can add an extra row if you want to create a bigger headband.

Function fewer rows here to make a smaller headband.

Bring in the active loop to a safety pin or stitch marker.

Switch the job and go back to the side with the starting chain to make the other half of the headband.

Row 21: Take a loop and ch 2 with the yarn connected to the skein. Work back through the start chain and work 1 hdc in the free band of each st in the string.

Total = 9 sts hdc.

Rows 22-26: Rep lines 2-6.

Row 27: Increase by one stitch at the beginning of the section. To do this, work 2 hdcs into the bl of the first st. In this line and in the rest of the pattern, make your increases like this. Finish the rest of the row by working hdc in each st in the row after through. Total = 10 M. Total.

Row 28: Job hdc in any st by block = 10 m in a row.

Row 29: Increase by one stitch at the beginning of the line. Total = 11 m in rows.

Row 30: Function hdc over every st by block = 11 m in a row. Row 30:

Row 31: Increase by one stitch at the beginning of the section. Total = row 12 sts.

Row 32: In through st, function hdc via blo = 12 meters in section.

Row 33: Increase by one stitch at the beginning of the line. Overall = 13 m in row.

Row 34: In each line, job hdc by blo = 13 sts in row.

Row 35: Increase by one stitch at the beginning of the range. Total = 14 m in rows.

Rows 36-40: Function hdc in each st by block = 14 m in each row.

If, in the first half of the project, you added additional rows after row 20, please add the same number of rows at the end too.

In your active loop, place a safety pin or stitch marker.

If the headband is not a gift, you can easily check and make sure that the checks are all right. Secure the sides of the headband with safety pins and put it on the intended recipient. Make some changes until the headband is done.

Finish the headband and keep together the two ends of the headband and secure it with a slip stitch. You may also use a whip stitch or other form of connection. Weave in ends.

Optional: You can apply slip stitches to both borders if you want to make the upper and lower edges of the belt look cleaner and done. The slip stitches do not stretch far, however, so the fit is affected. If you want to add your slip stitches, add them and work with loose, simple tension before tying the yarn.

10. Fingerless Gloves

This pattern is great if you want to wear an easy, fingerless pair of gloves and also a great last-minute gift. These gloves work well for those who want to donate their work to support others, even for a fast charitable crochet project.

Materials

This yarn is a number "3" in the yarn weight scheme of the Craft Yarn Board. Alternative weight names are "DK," "double knitting," or "light worsted." in all sizes. One 5, 00 oz / 140 g Bernat Softee ball (length: 362 yd / 331 m) is more than appropriate in all these gloves.

If you want to add another yarn for the small sizes and larger sizes, you need an average of 45 meters per 50 meters of identical yarn. Please notice this is an estimation only. Please ensure that plenty of yarn is not depleted.

Crochet hook: Using G/6 size — 4.25 mm crochet hook tapestry needle or needle for yarn: you need an eye needle that is wide enough to thread your yarn. It also helps to twee the ends while stitching the sides of the fingerless gloves together. You can also consider a needle threader useful, although it is not required.

Pattern and Gage

- ✓ Add Treble Crochet and a 3-gage chain is not necessary on these gloves but changes in size and fit.
- ✓ Stitch gage affects glove length. Change the chain number of chains to make the gloves longer or shorter.

Row gauge affects glove width and thickness. Set the number of rows to the appropriate size.

Instructions

Models Ch 30:

Row 1: tr in the fourth ch from the hook and st around the base side. Ch 3, transform.

Row 2: Function 1 tr over a row in an st. Ch 3, transform.

Rep row 2 before roughly one piece of steps. 6 1/8 inches, whatever you like.

Gloves Size

More or fewer rows Add Treble Crochet Rows, Calculate the diameter of your hand (or the hand from your intended user) at the maximum point over your thumb but below your finger to decide the size of the gloves you want to create.

If you use a stretchy yarn, like wool, you might want to make your gloves smaller than the actual measurements on your hand; the yarn is stretched out enough to fit comfortably.

Extra small for adult size: rep row 2 until piece fits approx. 6 1/8 inches, whatever you like.

Small / medium for adults: rep row 2 until piece measures around 7 cm.

For adults medium/large: rep row 2 up to around 7 7/8 inches in height.

Check the fit: it is helpful to fit quickly until the gloves are done. In the active loop, place a safety pin and then tie the sides of the glove together to see if it suits the specified wearer's hand.

Finishing Fingerless Gloves

When you are satisfied with fits, you are finished, leaving a 24-inch thigh of yarn that you use to thread your gloves 'side seams.

If you want to cover your gloves, it is time now. There is no need to block, but if you use wool yarn or intend to give them to a friend as a gift, it is a pleasant touch.

Assemble the Fingerless Gloves

Fold the rectangle to the top. Use the whip stitch to insert the top on the side of the gloves. Process the tapestry needle with the 24-inch yarn handle.

Place the flat glove in half to match the top and bottom sides.

Start stitching the whip in the corner. If you are right-handed, stitch from right to left. Stitch from left to right if you are left-handed.

Go through 6, 7, or roughly 2 inches and then leave a space for the thumb hole.

Reinforce the ends of the thumb hole. Reinforce the opening of the thumb by stitching the same stitch many times. There is a lot of wear and tear on the thumb opening, so this step is necessary.

Keep whip stitching around the piece in the same direction, but thread just one side through. Go through 8 or 9 stitches or 2 1/2 inches.

Sew a few more stitches at the other end of the thumb opening for more reinforcement at the same location.

To finish the gloves, continue the whip-stitching through both fabrics.

Follow these measures to complete the other glove again. Before weaving in your ends, make sure they suit each other.

When you finish the stitching and gloves, weave the remaining ends in the work so that they are safe and covered.

Now you can wear or tie your new gloves like a personalized gift that will bring comfort and joy.

11. Men's Scarf Crochet Pattern

Materials

This is the material you need to finish these men's crochet scarves.

- ✓ Yarn 200 g of DK / light weighted wool yarn Knit Picks Swish DK is used for the study at Lost Lake Heather.

✓ Crochet hook Length K/6.5 mm Change the appropriate gauge if necessary.

Measurements: 16 stitches and 28 rows = 4 in/10 cm in pattern

Row measurement is not important, but how much yarn you use can be changed. Unless you have the exact size of the finished scarf, make sure your swatch a gage and fit this recommended scale.

Finished Length: Around 75 cm long and 5 cm tall; by adjusting the length of your starting chain, you can change the thickness. The distance can also be conveniently changed by working more or fewer sheets.

Instructions

Scarf Crochet Men's Winter Pattern Ch 301:

Note: You can use stitch markers to mark every 25 stitches to help you keep track of such a long starter chain. Do not worry if you are a few chains off; this is a versatile design. If you do not care about the exact length, this suits the specified length, and you do not need to have an exact count.

Row 1: sl st in 2nd ch from the hook and around the row in each ch st. Row 2: Ch 1, turn.

Row 2: Ch 1, turn.

Row 3: Ch 1, transform. Job whole row in sl st. (300 mts.)

Row 4: Ch 1, switch. Job whole row at sl st (300 sl sts). Functions in the whole row in sc.

Row 5: Ch 1, turn. Row 5: Ch 1, turn. Perform the whole row in sl st from the row below in FRONT LOOP ONLY.

Row 6: Ch 1, transform. Row 6: Ch 1, transform. Function entire row in sl st.

Row 7: Ch 1, transform. Function whole row in sl st.

Row 8: ch 1, transform. Functions in the whole row in sc.

Repeat rows 5-8 until your sharp is as high as you like. To maintain the balance of your scarf, make sure it ends with 3 sl st rows.

Crochet SC and Slip Stitch Finish Scarf

Finish and weave in ends. If needed, block.

Do you want to add an additional finish?

In matching yarn or fabric, add fringe.

Join some snowflakes to make a nice snowy look.

The shell stitch works for a scarf that every little girl likes instead of a fringe at the top!

12. Fall Crochet Bunting

Materials

- ✓ Size 4 yarn in 2 colors: size J/6.0 mm
- ✓ Crochet hook
- ✓ Yarn
- ✓ Needle scissors

Gauge: 4 "size = 13 dc finished size: each rectangle has 4.5" long x 6.25 'tall designs. I prefer to crochet tightly. Since this is not a wearable object, if your size varies and your rectangles turn out to be slightly larger or smaller than mine, it will not be as big a deal.

However, if you crochet looser than me, your rectangles can be a little more "floppy" than mine. If so, you may want to down one or two sizes with your crochet hook to get the fabric you need.

Instructions

There will be slight curling of the rectangles, regardless of what the length is. Before I go on, I would suggest blocking your rectangles.

Growing row's start chain does not count as a stitch.

I refer to the main color of Color A and the complementary color of Color B in the 3 lines.

Row 1: Use Color A, 14 fdc OR (unless you want double crochet foundation) Chain 16. Dc through the third chain of the hook and through each row.

Row 2: Ch 1. (14) Row 2: Transform. Sc in the same thread and in every line. (14) Color switches B and Color A are done.

Row 3: Ch 1. Switch. Switch. Turn. Sc in one stitch and around each thread. Switch to Color A and full Color B. (14)

Row 4: Ch 2. Row 4: Switch. Turn. Dc in the same thread and throughout every line. Switch to Color B and full Color A.

Row 5: Ch 2. Switch. Turn. Dc in one row and around each thread. Color A shift and Color B finish. (14)

Row 6: Ch 2. Switch. Turn. Dc in the same thread and throughout every line. Color B and Color A finish off.

Row 7: Ch 1. Switch. Turn. Sc in one stitch and around each thread. Switch to Color A and full Color B. (14) Color A completes the rest of the pattern.

Row 8: Ch 1. Switch. Turn. Sc in one stitch and around each thread.

Row 9: Ch 2: Transform. Dc in the same thread and throughout every line. (14)

Rows 10-15: Rows 8 and 9 repeats. (14) Complete and weave all your ends.

Note: to prevent your color changing from loosening at the end of each row; I discreetly tied ends together in a small node before weaving.

If your corners curl, I would suggest that the rectangles be blocked before moving on to the next step.

Attach the rectangles: keep together two strands of color A, start crocheting a row. This beginning part of the chain (before the first rectangle is attached) can be made as long as you want. It depends on how your bunting is used. I have wired thirty for nine inches.

Put the first rectangle together with the two strands of color A on the top of the rectangle (14 stitches). Start chaining again after the last stitch of the rectangle. The length of your chain can be changed depending on the distance between your rectangles.

13. Color Block Bag Crochet Pattern

Materials

- ✓ U.S. H/5.00 mm Yarn DK (Light Worsted)
- ✓ Ultra Pima x 3 (Yellow Rose, Pink & Gray)-approx. Every color is 200 yards.

Finished size: 4 metal D-rings darning

This has a single crochet stitch around the tote top and is made from the Suzette stitch for the rest of the tote.

This color block bag is lightweight and easy to hold but is still large enough to accommodate anything you need.

Instructions

Pattern Color Chain 54 A:

Row 1: hook sc second row. Sc across the row in each thread.

Row 2–4: Sc across the row in each thread. Ch 1 and turn.

Rows 5–18: Sc, dc on the first row, * sc, dc on the next line, skip the row * repeat * to the end and end up with one crochet in the last line.

Row 19–36: Color shift B. Sc, dc in the first stitch, * sc, dc to next stitch, skip a stitch * repeat * until done, ending in the last stitch with one crochet.

Row 37–75: Color shift C. Sc, dc in the first stitch, * sc, dc to next stitch, skip a stitch * repeat * until done, ending in the last stitch with one crochet.

Row 76–92: Color shift B. Sc, dc in the first stitch, * sc, dc to next stitch, skip a stitch * repeat * until done, ending in the last stitch with one crochet.

Row 93–106: Color A transition. Sc, dc in the first stitch, * sc, dc to next stitch, skip a stitch * repeat * until done, ending in the last stitch with one crochet.

Row 107–110: Sc in each row stitch.

Cut the yarn, tissue in the ends.

This color block bag is lightweight and easy to hold but is still large enough to accommodate anything you need.

Finish: Fold the finished rectangle in half and seam up the two edges (the mattress stitch was used for attaching the bag edges).

Sew d-rings on the bag, using color A, approx. 1/2 "from the bag tip.

For each handle, crochet 2 i-cords; the through handle should be 18 "long or as long as you want. Stable D-ring i-cord with a double knot. If you do not know how to build an i-cord, check this helpful tutorial here.

14. Highland Ridge Pillow Free Crochet

Materials

- ✓ Product US model K/10.5 (6.5 mm)
- ✓ Crochet hook or crochet model to get a gage
- ✓ Yarn needle
- ✓ Scissors
- ✓ 18"pillow inserts (which are possible to buy or use my tutorial to make your own!)

The pattern in rows is figured out.

Instructions

1) Ch 2 will register as 1 FPdc at the beginning of even-numbered rows. Ch 2 is counted as 1 dc at the beginning of odd-numbered rows.
2) Job pattern for two parts twice.

Row 1 (RS): ch 48, 1 dc in 3rd ch from hook (1st ch counts as 1 dc), and 47 dc in each ch.

Row 2: Ch 2 (rate 1 FPdc) & switch, 1 FPdc per st in size – 47 FPdc.

Row 3: Ch 2 (counts 1 ft.) & transform 1 foot in every st – 47 foot.

Row 4-31: Rows 2-3 repeats.

Row 32: Section 2 repeats.

After row 32, add the first piece. After row 32, do not tighten and continue to finish the directions.

Finishing:

Keep the two pieces to reach the damaged ends. Continuing where you left the second piece at the end of row 32: ch 1, score equally on the three sides across the two pieces.

Please insert the pillow and continue along the fourth leg. Enter the 1st sc invisibly and fasten back.

15. Cross Body Bag Love

Materials

- ✓ Flikka in Birthday Cake H/5, 00 meters hook Tapestry 1 skein Lion Brand tapestry needle and scissors.
- ✓ **For furnishing:** fabric, needle, and thread, Faux leather body strap Color: smooth camel (gold clasp) Design notes 1 Lion Brand Re-up yarn can be used for this bag too.

Instructions

Unique stitch: Changed bead stitch works as follows: dc, * YE, just insert the hook (as though you operate on a front post dc), pull a loop, repeat three times from *, YO, pull through 9 crochet loops.

Chains do not count as a stitch at the beginning of each round.

Dimension finished: 9 "inches across.

Pattern 1: Magical ring, ch 2, 12dc in the ring, join first ft Round 2: Ch 2, * block st, ch 1, repeat from * at each ft around, add first bead stitch in round (you are attached to the dc part of the bead st) Round 3: Ch 2, ft in every ft around, join to first ft Note: each st will be 3 st-ft, each st worked around the dc, and the ch 1 round 4: ch 2, * block st, ch 1, sk 1, repeat fro

Create another circle.

Join the two circles together by crocheting the perimeter together while keeping the two circles together with the right sides. Leave 20 stitches for opening uncrocheted.

Change opening by crocheting more / less to make the opening of the bag smaller / larger.

Weave in ends. Turn inside so that the circles are facing outside on the right sides.

Add lining with the following directions.

Add a fake leather strap to either side of the opening of the case, ensuring that it fastens a complete stitch and not just a string of yarn.

Lining the Bag

Lay beneath the bag two bits of cloth. You can do that by piling the fabric halfway around the back of the fabric. Track around the bag, leaving an excess of around 1/2 inch. Label the textile where your opening starts and ends.

Cut out your bits of cloth.

The right side of the bits of fabric will face each other. Use thread and needle to sew around the loop or sew around with a sewing machine. Use a running point (going back and forth) to stitch the circle while you are using a needle and thread. Remember, we added approximately 1/2 inch additional fabric so you could sew this room. Leave the section where the opening was labeled unsewn.

Hold the back of the fabric outwards, placing it in the bag. Change to match the opening of the lining to open the crochet bag.

Fold the fabric carefully about 1/2 inch around the opening and pin to the crochet pocket. This helps the raw edge between the lining and the bag to be covered.

Conclusion

This guide has presented you with the crochet basics and if you have ever wanted to learn how to crochet, this tutorial is a great place to start. You will learn how to work different types of stitches and you will be able to create your own beautiful pieces.

Crochet is a fun and relaxing craft and what's also great is that it's easy to learn. It's a wonderful way to make your own stylish and cozy accessories. Your friends and family will love their gifts made by you and a handmade gift will remain a treasured keepsake.

Crochet can be a very pensive hobby and allows you to work on something that when finished, will bring you a great deal of satisfaction.

There is nothing stopping you from learning how to crochet and picking up your own yarn and hook! It really isn't that difficult. You will be so proud of yourself and all your creations too. So, go ahead and give it a try, you'll be so glad that you did.

One valuable tip is that you take your time while crocheting. The quality of your work will look nicer and more professional if you take your time. I use a lot of photos to help me plan out how to work a section before I start it or after I finish it. I also use pictures to make sure that I have everything the right way the first time.

I hope you enjoy the patterns, especially those of you that are new to crocheting. You can also try creating your own design from photos, magazines, and books.

All that's left now is for you to follow the instructions we covered here, use this guide as a reference and before you know it you'll be crocheting like a pro! Now it's time to get started.

I hope that this has been helpful in getting you started. Keep at it, you will soon be a crochet expert. Good Luck!

CPSIA information can be obtained
at www.ICGtesting.com
Printed in the USA
BVHW011249200821
614775BV00020B/102